DEALING DEATH AND DRUGS

THE BIG BUSINESS OF DOPE IN THE U.S. AND MEXICO

DEALING
DEATH
AND
DRUGS

THE BIG BUSINESS OF DOPE
IN THE U.S. AND MEXICO

An Argument to End the Prohibition of Marijuana

BETO O'ROURKE AND SUSIE BYRD

Cinco Puntos Press
EL PASO, TEXAS

FIRST EDITION
10 9 8 7 6 5 4 3 2 1

Library of Congress Cataloging-in-Publication

O'Rourke, Beto.
 Dealing death and drugs: the big business of dope in the U.S. and Mexico (an argument for ending the prohibition of marijuana) / by Beto O'Rourke and Susie Byrd. — 1st ed.
  p. cm.
 Includes bibliographical references.
 ISBN 978-1-933693-94-1 (alk. paper)
 1. Drug legalization—United States. 2. Drug traffic—Mexican-American Border Region. 3. Drug control—Mexican-American Border Region. 4. Marijuana industry—Mexico. 5. Marijuana industry—United States. 6. Narco-terrorism—Mexico. I. Byrd, Susannah Mississippi, 1971- II. Title.
 HV5825.O76 2011
 363.450973—dc23

2011034450

Cover and book design by Anne M. Giangiulio

The cover photograph (© 2010 by *El Paso Times*) is by Jesus Alcazar and is provided to Cinco Puntos Press as a courtesy by the *El Paso Times*. Caption: *Family members and friends gather at the gravesite of Sergio Adrian in the graveyard Garden of Memories in Ciudad Juárez* (10/06/10).

A portion of the proceeds from the sale of *Dealing Death and Drugs* will be donated to Centro Santa Catalina, a faith-based community in Ciudad Juárez, Mexico, founded in 1996 by Dominican Sisters for the spiritual, educational and economic empowerment of economically poor women and for the welfare of their families. centrosantacatalina.org

DEDICATED TO THE PEOPLE OF THE BORDER.

Thanks to Cinco Puntos Press, Lee, Bobby and Johnny Byrd. Thanks to those who read the initial manuscript and whose comments greatly improved the quality of the book: Molly Molloy, Debbie Nathan, Sito Negron, Vanessa Johnson, Dr. Richard Pineda and Mike Stevens. Thanks to Dr. Tony Payan and Karla Guevara who helped track down valuable information.

★ TABLE OF CONTENTS

INTRODUCTION
2008
WAS
DIFFERENT

El Paso sits on the Rio Grande, aka the U.S./Mexico border, across from Ciudad Juárez. I was born here. My co-author Susie Byrd moved to El Paso with her family when she was seven. Each of us grew up a few minutes from the river and Ciudad Juárez—this experience is the lens through which we write this book.

This is where Latin America and North America meet to form the largest binational community in the world. It's the point at which the 400-year-old Camino Real del Tierra Adentro—after having passed through Mexico City, Durango, Chihuahua and Juárez—crosses into present-day U.S. territory, continuing north through El Paso and on to Santa Fe, New Mexico.

This book is about what happens in our community when the value of the drugs that move through this ancient trade corridor exceeds the value of human life. We will explore the economy of the illegal drug trade, with a focus on that drug the cartels find most important to their bottom line: marijuana. With first person accounts, court transcripts and federal data, we will demonstrate how this simple weed has become the center of a multi-billion dollar industry. This industry is powerful enough to threaten governments, command horrifying violence and inspire the creation of outsized laws and budgets in the U.S., laws which end up strengthening the very cartels they were created to put out of business. We conclude by reviewing a previous experiment with prohibition and offer a solution that can undermine the power of the cartels and produce positive outcomes for both the U.S. and Mexico.

★

At first drive through, El Paso can feel like a richer, if more staid, suburb of Juárez, and Juárez can feel like a more exciting, if poorer suburb, of El Paso. El Paso has the tall downtown bank buildings, the ordered system of freeways and streets, the manicured lawns in distinct subdivisions. Juárez has the street life, the staggering swings between rich and poor and the invigorating chaos of 350 years of ad-hoc construction and twisting streets named for ghosts of the revolution. Bob Dylan sings about Juárez; El Paso gets Marty Robbins.

But the cities have each other. El Paso is over 500 miles from the Texas state capital and light-years from Washington D.C.; Juárez is the same distance, for all practical purposes, from Mexico's centers of power and population. So far away from the interest and focus of the state or feds, isolated from other major cities by hundreds of miles of barren desert plateau, the conjoined communities have long relied on each other in the development of their commerce, families and culture.

The vast majority of El Paso is of Mexican descent. If charted, the family trees of most would show ancestors from Juárez and other, smaller cities of the frontier state of Chihuahua. Cross-border family reunions are a common, daily affair, taking place in both Juárez, and especially these days, El Paso.

There is a distinct Spanish spoken in El Paso, *pocho*, inflected with code-switched local phrases that I heard and spoke as I grew up. I only learned later in El Paso High Spanish class that *ay te watcho* is not the proper way to take leave of one's friend.

While not a perfect melting pot, El Paso has long been a remarkably tolerant community. Many of my friends in grade school were first- or second-generation U.S. citizens whose families crossed over from Mexico. Others were Mexican citizens and claimed residency at the home of El Paso relatives or family friends in order to attend school here. The distinction between Anglo- and Mexican-American stood out (as do all distinctions at that age), but it was a distinction that lacked enough difference or meaning to determine who would or would not become a friend.

All of us spent time in Juárez. When we were young, we'd go to the markets and restaurants with our parents. As we got older, it was the nightclubs and bars. And when we were adults, it was back to the restaurants and markets with our own kids. Juárez was a destination for pleasure and fun, a place to take visitors to gawk and be entertained and then go home. You drank beer for 50 cents a bottle, bought some trinkets at the market and maybe walked by the old cathedral. Having to pay your way out of a real or imagined traffic violation was about the worst that could happen.

Growing up, I would hear about drug busts on the news, but it was such a common occurrence that it tended to blend into the background. Like the weatherman forecasting sunshine. While there is a rich history of black market trafficking in Juárez, going back at least to the U.S. alcohol prohibition of the 1920s, as a child I didn't understand or make the connection between the city next door and the news about drugs. If I ever did, it was only with the most passing of interests.

The news reports of cocaine or marijuana seizures were at times followed by one of a number of anti-drug commercials whose tag lines

I can still remember (e.g. "This is your brain on drugs," or "I learned it from watching you, dad!"). In hindsight, their ineffectiveness is obvious.

But at the time it was not something I paid much attention to, since I didn't use drugs and I wasn't interested in the subject. This was not the case for all of my friends though.

Some friends tried drugs, or at least had enough working knowledge of drugs to convince the rest of us that they knew what they were talking about. I remember a seventh-grade classmate at Mesita Elementary who not only bragged about getting high, but was caught selling dope to a janitor. He was the exception. Most kids I knew didn't try pot until later, when it was offered to them at high school parties or while drinking in the functionally all-ages bars of Ciudad Juárez.

As I grew older and listened to the news a little more carefully, I learned that Juárez was the crossing point for many of the drugs—and certainly all of the dope—sold and used in El Paso. Every so often there would be news of another big bust; tons of marijuana interdicted at the border coming over from Juárez or bundles of cash and cocaine uncovered in a stash house in El Paso. The sheer tonnage and enormous street value of these interdictions made it obvious that the Juárez/El Paso land port was an important logistical hub in the North American drug trade. But I didn't think that it affected me, so I didn't pay much attention.

In college, marijuana was even more available than it had been in high school. People smoked openly at parties, in dorm rooms and out on the streets.

Given everything that has happened in Juárez in the last few years, the fact that it is now the deadliest city in the world and the focus of the combined drug interdiction efforts of the U.S. and Mexico, it amazes me how little I knew or cared about these issues before. Having lived 35 years of my life within the front lines of the declared drug war; having seen drug use around me since middle school; having known that billions of dollars in drugs were transiting through my community...

until 2008 I can't remember ever thinking about drug policy, much less caring about it.

★

Violent death isn't a new phenomenon in Juárez. I can remember spasms of killings in Juárez that would temporarily halt the flow of El Pasoans crossing the international bridges in search of cosmopolitan restaurants, frenetic street life, cheap booze and the unquestioned welcome for school kids and GIs who wanted to get their rocks off.

But these cycles of violence, for those of us who were only indirectly affected, were treated like an intermittent natural phenomenon. Like the weather. It would be bad for a little while, and then get better. And what made it even easier to keep as an abstraction and not let it get to you was the convenient assumption that it only affected bad people, those who were involved in the drug trade.

2008 was different.

For the 15 years before 2008, the average number of murders per year in Juárez was 236. The murders of 316 people in 2007—the most in decades—produced a level of anxiety in the Juárez community that was unseen even during the femicides of the 1990s, when hundreds of women were abducted and murdered.

So when 1,623 people were murdered in 2008 the number was outside of anyone's realm of reference or possibility.

2008 was different in another way. People weren't just murdered: they were brutalized. Tortured. Maimed. Shot. Knifed. Strangled. Set on fire. Hanged. Dismembered. Beheaded. One at a time. 1,623 times in all.

But perhaps the most shocking distinction provided by the carnage of that year was not the number or manner of killings, but just who was being killed.

Not only were young and middle-aged men dying—the presumed

profile of the cartel workforce—so were women, pregnant mothers, the elderly and young children. No one was spared, and everyone, it seemed, was a potential victim.

The news media and the governments of Mexico and the U.S. were telling us that this spike in violence was linked to two wars that had just been announced. The first was President Felipe Calderón's war against the cartels. The second was Chapo Guzman's war against the Juárez cartel for control of the valuable transit route leading from Juárez into El Paso and the rest of the U.S. drug market, valued between $63 and $81 billion.

At first these two narratives made it easy to dismiss the awful bloodshed as nothing more than settled scores amongst cartels. While hard to prove, since almost none of the murders were ever solved, it made sense and fit nicely with the long-taken view in the region that as long as you were clean and steered clear of the drug trade, you had nothing to worry about. But as the numbers, details and circumstances of the victims became known, the conclusion was unavoidable: something new and tragic was taking place in Juárez, and it wasn't going to go away no matter how hard we tried to ignore it.

As if to reinforce the permanence of the problem, families, especially those with money and connections, began to trickle, and then stream, out of Juárez and into El Paso. They bought homes, enrolled their children in local schools and started businesses and new careers. By the end of 2008, the mayor of Ciudad Juárez himself was living safe and secure in El Paso, along with an estimated 30,000 other newly expatriated Juarenses.

The rate and brutality of the murders and reigning impunity in Juárez forced me to consider a number of questions. Why were "good" people dying as well as "bad" people? Could that distinction even be measured? And if it could, did it matter? More bluntly, did anyone deserve to die like this? And lastly, and most importantly, what role did I have in this?

As a fourth-generation El Pasoan, and since 2005, a member of the El Paso City Council whose 80,000-person district borders Mexico, I didn't want to sit by and witness all of this and do nothing. I wanted to understand and to act.

It became clear that this was not a simple problem. There were a number of contributing factors that one could point to, from the rapid industrialization of Juárez, a decades-long transformation that had attracted hundreds of thousands of people from the surrounding countryside to work in factories without the social and civic infrastructure to support them; to the absence of any true respect for the rule of law, expressed in the bribing of police and the obsequiousness paid to drug lords and leading patriarchs alike. Rule of the strong, and not the law, was seemingly bred into the bones of the city.

But there was perhaps an even more pernicious influence acting on Juárez in these years. The more I thought about it as the number of murdered rose in 2008, the clearer it became that Juárez was caught in a multibillion dollar hemispheric vice between supply and demand. North America consumes illegal drugs, Mexico supplies them. When there is interference between the supply and demand, people start dying.

At the same time that I was thinking about what city council could do to help, others in the city were working on these same questions, including the City of El Paso's Committee on Border Relations. Comprised of academic, business and government leaders, the group offered a resolution in response to the Juárez violence to the El Paso City Council for adoption in early 2009. It made a number of important policy recommendations including encouraging stronger interdiction efforts to stop the southbound guns and cash that armed and empowered the killers; encouraging Mexico to strengthen its institutions and respect for rule of law; and urging both countries to work harder to stop and treat drug use.

As the resolution was being presented to the City Council, I asked whether we should more aggressively address the issues related to demand and prohibition. I listened to the answers, followed the debate among my colleagues and then offered an amendment, composed on the spot, to encourage "an honest, open, national debate on ending the prohibition on narcotics."

It was an artless, and even inaccurate amendment to the larger resolution (I only learned later that marijuana is not a narcotic, even though it was precisely that drug that I felt people would be most open to debating), but it got the point across.

I knew we were addressing a taboo topic, one that conventional wisdom dictated that only potheads, hard-core libertarians and political suicides ever brought up. But I also knew that Juárez had gone well beyond the pale and it was time to place all options on the table, even those that had been unthinkable, for me as well as others, just a year ago.

The resolution, including the amendment I offered on an "honest, open" debate, passed unanimously. I was surprised. The eight of us (myself, Ann Lilly, Susie Byrd, Emma Acosta, Melina Castro, Rachel Quintana, Eddie Holguin and Steve Ortega) could rarely agree on anything, from setting the tax rate to whether or not we should have bike lanes—and yet, on one of the most politically charged topics in the nation, we were in unanimous agreement. It was testament to the fact that, despite our differences, we were all El Pasoans who understood at a basic level that our fellow *fronterizos* were dying, that the safety and welfare of the city we represented was under threat and that our long-term future was in doubt. We wanted to do something to make our voices heard, and voting for this nonbinding resolution became our opportunity.

Later in the day, Mayor John Cook surprised us by vetoing the resolution that he'd been mum on throughout the meeting where it had been debated. When confronted, he cited a concern that we'd be "laughed out of Austin and D.C." when we went begging for our allotment of state and federal funds.

I trusted that the leaders in our state and national capitals—and more importantly the people in El Paso—would understand that this was no laughing matter. I resolved to try to override the veto and placed it on the next Tuesday's city council agenda.

On the day before the vote, Council members began to receive calls from our congressman, Silvestre Reyes, chair of the powerful House Intelligence Committee. He asked us not to move forward with the resolution and delivered a thinly veiled threat: failure to do so would result in the withholding of stimulus funds for our city, the third poorest in the United States.

The question now was: would we have the courage of our convictions?

The Congressman's El Paso chief of staff, Sal Payan, addressed the council on the Congressman's behalf in the public meeting the next day. He reiterated the Congressman's vague threats and urged us to desist.

His efforts paid off. Six votes were needed to override the mayor's veto, and it became clear as we took a roll call vote that only four were sticking with their original votes.

Each of the Council members who folded cited the federal blackmail. City Representative Eddie Holguin, one of the most conservative members of the Council, said "I don't regret supporting the resolution…" but "…at this point I can't jeopardize funding from the state or the federal level."

It seemed that El Paso wasn't going to be able to change the terms of the drug war and take an active role in helping its sister city. We would need to leave it in the hands of the feds.

When asked what we could expect from the Congressman and the administration in D.C. going forward, the Congressman's spokesman tried to reassure us: "This thing is going to break in the next six months. It can't go any further. Believe me."

Of course, things didn't break in the next six months. They got much, much worse.

★ **Beto O'Rourke**

CHAPTER 1
WHY IS JUÁREZ THE DEADLIEST CITY IN THE WORLD?

Raul Xazziel Ramirez-Ramirez was seven years old when he was killed in Juárez.

He lived his short life there and in El Paso, one of hundreds of thousands of true *fronterizos* whose lives define the fluid nature of citizenship and nationality on the U.S./Mexico border. The cities are halves of one, large binational metropolis. And people, despite the border walls and onerous customs inspections at the ports of entry, still move relatively freely between the two sides.

The same year Raul was killed, 7 million pedestrians and cars crossed the international bridges that join the two cities. This despite 2009 being at that point the most violent year in the history of the region.

The dynamics are constant regardless of the violence. Juarenses come north to shop (spending close to $1.5 billion each year in El Paso), to work and to visit family and friends. Then, for the most part, they go back home.

El Pasoans cross to the south, just not as often as they used to. Now it is largely limited to those who own small businesses in Juárez or work within the large maquila industry that dominates the official economy of Juárez.

Many children leave their immediate family in Juárez to attend school in El Paso while staying with a relative. Raul stayed with his aunt during the school week and attended Glen Cove Elementary in east El Paso.

The night he was killed—November 13, 2009—was a Friday, and Raul was back in his hometown, his dad driving the two of them through the Anapra neighborhood, one of the poorest in Juárez, overlooking the Rio Grande, which forms the political boundary between the two countries.

Whatever they were talking about—Raul's grades, how he was liking life in El Paso, the movie he wanted to see that weekend—was brutally interrupted as their car was approached by another. Gunmen inside the second car opened fire, the bullets ripping through glass and metal and into his father's head and chest, killing him as he sat next to his son.

As their white Suzuki rolled to a stop in the midst of what is usually a busy traffic circle, Raul opened the door and ran for his life.

The gunmen had stopped their car as well, and after confirming that his father was dead, pursued Raul and shot him with a 9 mm gun, the bullets landing squarely in his back. He fell to the ground, crawling away from the gunmen before dying a few hundred feet from El Paso.

★

Hundreds of children like Raul have been murdered in Juárez since Mexican President Felipe Calderón declared war on organized crime gangs in 2008. Some were killed as they tried to flee; others were strangled or shot to death as they slept. We assume they were not the primary targets; their fathers, mothers, aunts, uncles, older cousins and relatives were. But their deaths were not incidental.

Their city is now the deadliest in the world, and has carried this notorious distinction approaching three years in a row. In 2009, the 2,754 murders resulted in a rate of 165 murdered per 100,000 residents. In 2010, it rose to 200 people per 100,000 residents as total killings increased and the number of residents in the city decreased by tens of thousands. Upwards of 100,000 Juarenses abandoned their homes, jobs and businesses for a safer life deeper in the interior or across the border.

One of the safe havens that these families run to is El Paso, Texas, which shares a 20-mile contiguous border with Juárez. It's a city bound to Juárez by deep and unbreakable historical, familial, economic and cultural ties. Businessmen and gangsters who rule over empires in Juárez by day sleep in El Paso at night, their children attending the best private schools in the city. And yet El Paso is the safest city of its size in the United States. By the end of 2010, there had been 3,111 murders in Juárez.[3] In El Paso, there had been five.

The conventional explanation for the hell that had engulfed Juárez, offered by Mexican President Felipe Calderón and many in the U.S. government, was that the killings were the result of internecine and intercartel struggles and that, essentially, those who had been killed were guilty of participation in the illegal drug market.

"If you're clean, you have nothing to worry about," went a common response to those who were concerned about the escalating violence. Even the killing of a seven-year-old boy like Raul could be explained away as the unavoidable result of his father's assumed involvement in the drug trade.

The problem with the conventional explanation was that it wasn't supported by the facts, which, with a complete breakdown of law enforcement and the judiciary, were hard to come by. In 2010, suspects had been identified in only 3 percent of the over 3,000 murders committed.

The truth is no one knows for sure why people are killing people at such an alarming rate in Juárez because only very rarely is a murder solved and the murderer prosecuted.

This idea that not all dead are guilty exploded into the national consciousness in early 2010 after the Villas de Salvarcar massacre, when 13 children were murdered at a birthday party held at a private home. Calderón initially dismissed the murdered children as thugs involved in the drug trade.

As evidence mounted that, in fact, the victims were honor students and athletes, the president was forced to admit that he was wrong. While addressing the parents of the slain students in Juárez, he said, "It is clear… that the boys were role models, athletes, students, good students and good children."[4]

After this, Mexicans were no longer able to comfort themselves with the thought that the murders, tortures and mutilations were perpetrated on "the guilty" alone. For if that had been the case, then Mexico would be justified in continuing to prosecute its war on organized crime and Mexicans and Juarenses could continue to believe, or hope, that it was only the "enemy"—the guilty, the dirty—who had to fear the brutality and grotesque carnage occurring in the homes, restaurants, office buildings, rehab clinics, streets, sidewalks and alleys of Juárez throughout every day and every night of the terrible years, 2008, 2009, 2010 and now 2011.

★

With a city government that could not protect its citizens, much less bring justice to those who had been murdered, Juárez was left to confront the implications left by the evidence.

Clearly, there was a strong relation between the violence and the black market drug trade. Billions of dollars in drugs are staged in Juárez and crossed into the United States via the ports of entry in El Paso every year. There was a declared war between the two largest regional operators—the Juárez cartel and the Sinaloa cartel—for primacy in this *plaza*, which essentially meant control of the cross-border corridors, the local police and the logistics of the transborder drug trade in Juárez. The war was advertised and reported by the cartels themselves: in the messages hung on or carved into the bodies of their victims, and in the narco *mantas* (banners) hung on buildings and freeway overpasses.

Just as clearly, there was a relation between Calderón's declared war on the drug cartels and the violence. In 2007, a year after he declared war and a year before he sent 2,500 army troops and 425 federal police to Juárez, there were 320 murders in Juárez, a 40 percent increase over the average number for the last five years and cause for considerable concern at the time.

As 2008 opened, it was obvious that things were getting worse at an alarming rate. In January, 46 people were killed, double the monthly average for 2007. In February, 49 killed. In March, 117.

In response to the increasing violence, Calderón sent the army and federal police into Juárez at the end of that month. This initially seemed to provide the desired effect. April reported only 55 dead.

Then May, 136 dead.

June, 139 dead.

July, 146 dead.

By the end of 2008, 1,623 people were murdered in Juárez.

The numbers showed a surprising inverse correlation between the active role of the federal government in pursuing the drug cartels and the public safety of Juárez. This was confirmed the following year when more federal police were deployed to Juárez at the end of February 2009. Again things cooled for a month or so, and then the killings surpassed the already surprising rate of the previous year. 2009 ended with the murder of 2,754 people. And, instead of "breaking," as Congressman Reyes had assured El Paso it would in 2009, the violence only continued to escalate. The following year, in 2010, 3,111 people were murdered.

The institutions that form and protect a civil society, the ones most Americans take for granted—the courts, the police, the government— were ineffective and even counterproductive in Juárez. The public's safeguards were rotted with corruption by years of collaboration with the cartels in moving illegal product to the United States and weakened by a lack of trust and respect from the public. The public institutions stood in desperate need of repair or even a complete rebuilding.

This had been exacerbated by years of migration from the Mexican interior to Juárez and other border communities, cities that had been quickly industrialized to serve the North American market. Rural poor who had no experience living outside of their small towns and villages were now living in a cutthroat center of capitalism, with little governmental, social or familial support to mitigate the negative effects or provide opportunities for a better life. The *Economist* reported in 2002 that during this time of rapid industrialization and population growth, the outskirts of Juárez:

> …became sprawling slums. Now 175,000 residents have no running water, 140,000 lack sewerage and only half the city's 1,200 miles (1,920 kms) of roads are paved. And little money has gone into training a better workforce. On the city's west side, where 500,000 people live in some of Mexico's most squalid slums, the only two high schools have a drop-out rate of 95 percent.[5]

During 2010, it also became clear that not only were victims not always members of drug gangs, as with the Villas de Salvarcar murders, but that the perpetrators could not be explained away as cartel assassins.

It became apparent that many crimes of opportunity were occurring as the city became more inoculated to violence, as the price of life cheapened, and as the message became clear to the tens of thousands of *ninis* (*ni trabajan, ni estudian*—young men who had neither employment nor schooling) that violence was a means for advancement, for obtaining wealth and for settling scores. And that furthermore, violence would not be punished by the government.

Gustavo de la Rosa Hickerson, Juárez Ombudsman for the Chihuahua State Human Rights Commission, described these crimes of opportunity in a 2010 interview:

> Now we estimate that there must be over 4,500 armed people who are prepared to kill. Many of them fourteen-, fifteen-year-old kids who hate the guy who stole their girlfriend, who hate the father who yelled at them, the teacher who flunked them, who hate the rival gang, and who, on top of that, have learned how to kill. So now we don't know if the homicides are in fact linked to the drug trade or if this is simply the most interesting manifestation of urban violence." [6]

The El Paso/Juárez trade corridor is essential to the North American economy. More than $70 billion in legal trade passed through regional ports of entry last year, almost 20 percent of all U.S./Mexico legal trade. El Paso/Juárez is the second largest trade corridor after Laredo on the U.S./Mexico border.

Like its legal counterpart, the Juárez corridor is a prized staging area for the North American black market.

From slaves bound for the underground U.S. sex trade to migrant farmworkers and maids headed for U.S. fields and subdivisions, Juárez is a logical point of entry for all manner of illicit commerce.

But it is the illegal drugs—marijuana, cocaine, heroin and methamphetamines—that make the plaza so valuable, worth fighting and dying for. And it is marijuana that is arguably the most valuable of all.

Marijuana, unlike almost anything else transited through Mexico, has a supply chain that is fully controlled by the cartels. They grow the product, pack it, transit it, cross it, and in many cases, control wholesale distribution all the way into North American markets. Marijuana has the largest customer base and most consistent demand in the United States. It is the cornerstone product of the criminal enterprises operating in Mexico, and of all the illegal goods trafficked through the Juárez plaza, it is the most critical to their bottom line.

★

The Juárez plaza was long controlled by what is commonly referred to as the Juárez cartel, or the Carillo Fuentes cartel, with its armed faction known as La Linea.

The Juárez cartel was founded by Amado Carrillo Fuentes in the early 1990s. Like many Mexican drug cartels, it increased in power and earnings as the power and earnings of the Colombian cartels decreased.

At its apex under Amado's leadership, the cartel controlled extensive trafficking territory in Mexico and along the U.S./Mexico border, and had a fleet of Boeing 727 jet airliners to facilitate the transit of Colombian cocaine throughout its network. It's also worth mentioning that the baseline, or "normal", murder rate of 230 murders per year was set around this time.

After Amado died in a botched plastic surgery operation, he was ultimately succeeded by his brother, Vicente Carrillo Fuentes.

Vicente was successful in creating temporary peace after the fractious battle to succeed his brother by allying with other drug cartels in the region, including the Beltran-Leyva organization and the Sinaloan cartel led by Joaquín "El Chapo" Guzmán Loera.

However, early in the past decade the relationship between Guzmán Loera and Carillo Fuentes began to fray as the Sinaloan cartel actively recruited converts from the Juárez organization. In 2004, Guzman Loera had his rival's brother murdered. Shortly thereafter, Carillo Fuentes returned the favor by ordering a successful hit on the brother of Guzman Loera.

The selective assassinations turned into open battle by 2007 as the Sinaloan cartel made an aggressive bid for the valuable Juárez plaza.

As the battle for Juárez raged, it was clear that one era of the plaza was ending and another beginning. The Juárez cartel was simply unable to capitalize on the gains made under the leadership of Amado Carrillo Fuentes and was largely in a position of maintaining turf or accommodating rising powers like the Sinaloan cartel.

In April of 2010, the *Associated Press* declared the fight over and the Sinaloan cartel the winner. The widely carried news article left many confused. How then to explain the increasing rate of violence? If Chapo had achieved victory, wouldn't violence decrease and some sort of Pax Sinaloa be established in Juárez? And why has the Juárez cartel been able to stage car bombs, assassinations and other displays of power? Instead, 2010 became the deadliest year yet, with more than 3,000 people murdered.

★

Felipe de Jesús Calderón Hinojosa was elected president of Mexico in 2006. Ten days after being sworn in, Calderón launched the current war against the drug cartels in Mexico by sending 6,500 troops to Michoacán.[7] Calderón vowed to go after the cartels at all levels, from the street dealers to the capos. After years of alternately praising Mexican cooperation and then bemoaning the lack of a true drug war ally in Mexico, the United States once again stated that it finally had a president upon whom it could depend.

Calderón moved away from eradication efforts and focused the army and federal police on direct combat with the cartels, earning plaudits and unstinting support from his admirers in the U.S. government.

As it became clear in early 2008 that the rate and brutality of killings in Juárez was reaching a politically untenable level, Calderón initiated Operation Chihuahua by sending 2,000 soldiers, 425 federal police officers and various investigative and intelligence operatives to the beleaguered city.

The operation commenced with a partial takeover of the local police operations, with a promise by then-Mayor José Reyes Ferriz to clean up the force, widely assumed to be involved in perpetrating much of the violence and facilitating drug trafficking in Juárez.

There was also a public relations battle being waged from Mexico City. Attorney General Eduardo Medina Mora became a spokesman for the drug war, espousing the view that the violence raging in Juárez and throughout much of northern Mexico was an indication of success against the cartels. He called the 5,000 murders that had taken place across Mexico from 2006 to 2008 a "sign of their weakness, decomposition and deterioration."[8]

Despite increased federal army and police levels, the firing of more than half of the presumed corrupt local police force[9] and a growing international notoriety for unabated violence and impunity, the pace of killings only increased. 2009 finished with 2,754 murders, 2010 with 3,111.

★

In just three years, violence had become a way of life in Juárez, the terror compounded by a frightful disintegration of institutions and social norms.

But what chance did Juárez have to reestablish these when the barbarity and terrorism were fueled by billions of dollars in drug proceeds and weapons funneled from the U.S.?

CHAPTER 2
PROFIT

In July 2010, the Chicago police, acting on a tip, staked out Francisco Gonzalez-Nieto. After observing Francisco in the middle of a drug deal, the police followed him home and found $70,000 in cash, 4,000 grams of cocaine and 1,900 pounds of marijuana, enough for 4,000 hits and almost 2 million joints. The police told the media that Francisco Gonzalez-Nieto was likely tied to drug-trafficking organizations in Mexico.

Chicago is one of the largest drug markets in the United States and one of the most lucrative destinations for illegal drugs flowing through the Juárez plaza. If you are getting high in Chicago today, chances are good that your drug of choice was imported from Mexico. Perhaps it came through Juárez.

In addition to controlling most of the supply of drugs into Chicago, Mexican drug cartels also dominate the wholesale distribution of cocaine, heroin and marijuana in the region and for many years have been considered by drug enforcement officials as the single greatest drug trafficking threat in the region.[10]

"Much like any legitimate corporation, the drug organizations utilize Chicago as both a distribution and trans-shipment point for their product. The extensive accessibility to various modes of transportation, as well as the large and diverse population with an established customer base, makes Chicago an ideal location as a hub," Stephen A. Luzinski, acting special agent-in-charge of the Drug Enforcement Agency in Chicago, told the *Washington Post* in a 2009 interview.[11]

★

It's hard to know exactly how much a drug-trafficking organization in Mexico stood to gain if Francisco hadn't been busted in Chicago. The cartels aren't members of the Chamber of Commerce, they aren't reporting their loads to Customs, they aren't reporting their income to the IRS, they aren't paying sales tax and they aren't interested in interviews.

Much of what we do know about the business of illicit drugs we know through law enforcement efforts. The Drug Enforcement Agency tracks the wholesale and retail price of drugs in large retail markets in the United States. In transit countries, they gather this information from drug seizures and undercover purchases. But it is difficult to get a full picture of drug market profitability because the DEA doesn't track and report expenses.

The other way to understand the profitability of the drug market is to ask the people who bring the drugs here. An incarcerated source within one of the cartels operating in Juárez provided details for pricing and logistics along the route from farm to market, in this case from Chihuahua to Chicago via the Juárez plaza. His information is descriptive of 2010 market activity and was checked, where possible, against U.S. federal enforcement data, court transcripts and reporting on the drug war to verify the reliability of the sources information.[12] Expenses and values were provided by the insider as a range. The following analysis uses the low end of the range.

FROM FARM TO JUÁREZ

The dominant area for marijuana cultivation in Mexico is the rugged terrain of the Western Sierra Madres in an area called the Golden

Triangle, which straddles the tri-state region of Sinoloa, Chihuahua and Durango.

Growers, either controlled by or affiliated with the different cartels, are paid about $23 per pound at the low end of the range, according to the cartel insider.[13]

For the 1,900 pounds of marijuana that Gonzalez-Nieto was busted with in Chicago, a cartel would have paid a farmer $43,700.

To own the right of free movement of illegal product through a locale in Mexico, drug cartels have negotiated a plaza (an exclusive franchise agreement) with law enforcement and political interests. A former Juárez police officer, testifying in a federal drug trial, described the plaza as having complete and exclusive control over law enforcement in a particular area. The control exercised through the plaza agreement gives the traffickers "free reign" to continue drug trafficking through the area without any interference from law enforcement, and in some cases, with the aid of law enforcement.[14]

Law enforcement, unlike many of the other actors in the drug trade, isn't paid on a per-load basis. They are paid regularly for the right of access regardless of how much product is moved through the area. The former Juárez police officer referred to these payments as "payroll," indicating that it was not a bribe but a payment for services. In return for the regular payment, the police officer is expected to do what the cartels ask.[15]

When questioned about what happens to police officers who refuse to be on payroll, the former Juárez police officer responded that even if a police officer is not on the cartel payroll, they would still be required to obey the orders given by the cartels. If a police officer decided not to obey orders, he would be killed.[16] The choice given to police officers is *plata o plomo*, silver or lead—money or bullets.

Some cartels take their chances with other routes. According to the insider, "others prefer to take it on the back roads and get it to the Juárez area without involving the law. There are even others that will pay mules…which is simply a guy they pay about $1,000 to carry a pack of 50 pounds from the mountains all the way across the border of the U.S. and drop it for someone to pick it up."

The driver who runs the pot from the farm to Juárez is paid about $14 a pound. For Gonzalez-Nieto's load, the driver made out with $26,600 for driving the 1,900 pounds from the mountains to Juárez via the highway. It is likely that the driver would be carrying more than just the 1,900 pounds. Because the route is protected by the plaza agreement and there is little risk of seizure, loads traveling through Mexico tend to be far larger than those traveling through the United States. Once the marijuana gets to Mexican border cities, like Juárez, it is broken into smaller quantities at stash houses for transport to the United States.[17]

According to the cartel source, "[It] depends on who the product belongs to but some of the product stays in Juárez for resale while some moves on to El Paso for resale while some gets loaded on trucks headed north." In Juárez, marijuana usually sells wholesale for $73 a pound at the low end. The 1,900-pound load that was purchased for $43,700 in the Golden Triangle would have been valued at $138,700 in Juárez.

FROM JUÁREZ TO EL PASO

One of the biggest risks in moving drugs to the U.S. market is in jumping the line from Mexico into the United States. Since 9/11, the federal government has dramatically increased enforcement and inspections at ports of entry and significantly increased the number of Border Patrol agents patrolling the line between ports of entry. In 2004, there were 10,000 Border Patrol agents. Today that number has increased to almost 21,000. Most of these agents are deployed along the southern border.[18]

Freight costs in the drug market are priced on risk. Cartels pay $40 a pound at the low end to $60 a pound to move marijuana five miles from Juárez to El Paso. This is almost three times as much as the cost of freight for moving marijuana hundreds of miles from the Golden Triangle to Juárez.

A broker is used to negotiate the crossing into El Paso. Yet another broker is used to negotiate the next stage of the shipment. Instead of a cartel selling and shipping directly to a client in Chicago, several brokers are employed to get it to its final destination. Great care is taken to make sure that no one person has much knowledge about other people involved in the transaction. This way, if one person gets arrested, he or she has limited information to give to law enforcement about other actors involved in the transaction.

The Juárez broker hires a driver, and when possible, a willing U.S. customs agent to facilitate the movement of the drugs through the ports of entry. The agent and the drivers are paid out of the $40 a pound for freight. For loads over 1,000 pounds, the customs agent will get $10 or less a pound. In the case of the load headed to Chicago, assuming it was crossed as one load through the port of entry and assuming it was crossed with the aide of a custom's agent, freight at $40 a pound would cost $76,000 with approximately $19,000 going to the customs agent.

The U.S. government recently convicted Martha Garnica, a U.S. Customs and Border Protection agent known to the cartels as La Estrella, for six counts of drug smuggling, human trafficking and bribery. As a customs agent, La Estrella directed the activities of five traffickers in order to ensure the safe passage of illegal drugs and undocumented immigrants. She was paid handsomely and actively recruited other customs agents to participate in facilitating the movement of illegal drugs through the ports of entry.

Juárez brokers use a variety of strategies for moving product across the line. "As far as crossing the border, about 50 percent is left to chance and 50 percent has a worked-out deal with either Customs or somebody to let it through without problems. Not all product crosses through the bridges. Some will cross through the Juárez valley across the river during shift changes or the same time out in the desert between El Paso and Columbus. Large loads of 1,000 pounds or more are hidden in semi-trucks of food and cargo. Other smaller loads will be hidden in trucks and cars crossed little by little. Some, just a few pounds at a time, will be strapped to the body of the mules walking across the bridge."

Halcones (hawks) are employed by the cartels to monitor the movements and patterns of the international trade through the ports of entry and to advise about the best times, routes and strategies to cross illegal loads. For example, halcones identify unsuspecting commuters who are able to move easily between the two cities because they have been identified by the U.S. government as trustworthy. The halcones then track their mark's daily travel patterns and locate the VIN number for the car. The cartels reproduce car keys based on the VIN number provided by the halcones and place illegal drugs in the vehicles of these unsuspecting motorists. Ana Isela Martinez, who commuted from Juárez to El Paso to teach fourth grade, spent six weeks in the infamous Cereso Prison in Juárez after Mexican troops found over a 100 pounds of marijuana in her trunk. It wasn't until the FBI broke the ring that had capitalized on her regular commuting habits that she was released from prison.

Once the marijuana gets to El Paso, it is valued at $240 a pound, or $456,000 for Francisco's load. Moving from one side of the border to the other increases the value of marijuana by three. In Juárez, Francisco's load was worth $138,700 but move it five miles north and it increases in value to $456,000.

Once the drugs make it to El Paso, they are typically transported to stash houses where they are consolidated, repackaged and shipped to markets nationwide. That's where the real profits are. Street values of drugs in El Paso are much lower than in larger markets where most of the product transited through Juárez is headed—Atlanta, Dallas/Fort Worth, Oklahoma City, Chicago, St. Louis and Denver.

The El Paso region's role in the drug trade is mostly limited to warehouse and distribution to other larger, more profitable American markets. This is similar to El Paso's role in the maquila sector, where goods are manufactured in Juárez then shipped to El Paso for distribution to U.S. markets. The relatively low value of the retail drug trade in El Paso might be one reason that the murder rate here is so low compared to other, more lucrative destination markets. The average murder rate for the previously mentioned cities was 16 murders per 100,000 in 2010; in El Paso it was 0.8 per 100,000.

FROM EL PASO TO CHICAGO

Mexican drug cartels are now the dominant wholesalers of illegal drugs in the United States, having expanded their role from selling to American wholesalers to setting up their own wholesale operations in important distribution hubs throughout the United States.[19] Law enforcement reports show that Mexican drug cartels are operating in 237 cities throughout the country. For marijuana, Mexican cartels effectively own the supply chain from farm to market.

The 1,900 pound load that landed Gonzalez-Nieto in prison in Chicago would cost $75 a pound to move to Chicago, or $142,500.

When the pot gets to Chicago, its wholesale value is $550 a pound. A load that was purchased for $43,700 in the Sierra Madres is now worth $1,045,000 in Chicago.

All of this value is added even before it is sold retail. The Chicago Police claimed that the street value of the 1,900 pounds of marijuana was over $5 million.

CARTEL MARKUP: FROM FARM TO MARKET

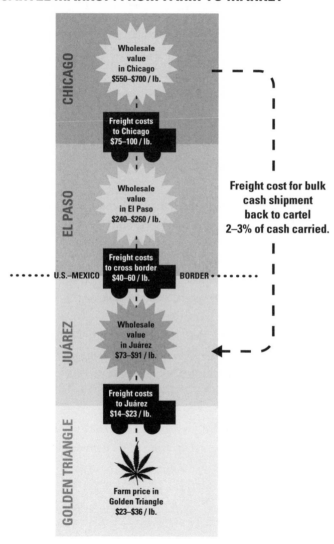

CHICAGO

Wholesale
value
in Chicago
$550–$700 / lb.

Freight costs
to Chicago
$75–100 / lb.

EL PASO

Wholesale
value
in El Paso
$240–$260 / lb.

Freight costs
to cross border
$40–60 / lb.

· · · · · · · U.S.–MEXICO   BORDER · · · · · · ·

Freight cost for bulk
cash shipment
back to cartel
2–3% of cash carried.

JUÁREZ

Wholesale
value
in Juárez
$73–$91 / lb.

Freight costs
to Juárez
$14–$23 / lb.

GOLDEN TRIANGLE

Farm price in
Golden Triangle
$23–$36 / lb.

BRINGING THE PROFITS HOME

Cash from drug transactions is consolidated in regional distribution hubs like Chicago and then sent back to Mexico through couriers. The cartel insider adds that "usually smaller amounts will be hidden in suitcases on buses and cars, while larger amounts get put on a semi-truck. When people are freighting money back south, the normal costs are 2 percent to 3 percent of the total amount brought."

If hired at 2 percent, a courier bringing back the money from Francisco Gonzalez-Nieto's transaction would be paid $20,900 to carry the $1,045,000 back to Mexico.

If Francisco Gonzalez-Nieto hadn't been caught, the 1,900 pound load would cost about $309,700 at the low end to get from farm to market and to return the cash to the cartel. The wholesale value of this load in Chicago would be $1,045,000 for a profit of $735,300. This is a return on investment of 237 percent.

At the high end of the cartel insider's estimates, the load would cost about $456,000 and would be sold for $1,330,000 in Chicago for a profit of $874,000. This is a return on investment of 192 percent.

This incredible profit margin allows the cartels to pay for the police protection, the corrupt judiciary and politicians and the hitmen. It more than makes up for the significant losses incurred when loads are interdicted at the border or later in the supply chain, as in the case of Gonzalez-Nieto in Chicago.

★

The Rand Drug Policy Research Center looked at the impacts on the price of marijuana if cartels were removed from the equation by legalizing the cultivation, production, distribution and possession of marijuana in California. They determined that high-grade marijuana that is available in an illegal market today for $375 an ounce would be sold for $38 an ounce pre-tax in a legal market, assuming "typical producer and retailer markups of 25 percent and 33 percent, respectively, and allowing an additional $40 per pound for logistics and distribution."[20] Their analysis demonstrates that the prohibition of marijuana accounts for 90 percent of the markup of marijuana.

Using the black market markup revealed in the Rand Report, Francisco Gonzalez-Nieto's 1,900 pound load of Mexican marijuana—valued by the Chicago police at $5 million retail in a black market—would be worth only $507,000 in a legal economy.

CHAPTER 3
DEMAND

The U.S. is the most valuable illegal drug market in the world. Recent estimates put the total value of illegal drug markets in the U.S. at between $63 and $81 billion.[21]

The size and value of the marijuana market seems to elicit the largest range in estimates. Depending on who you talk to, the value of the market ranges from $11 billion to $113 billion annually.[22]

Policymakers in the U.S. and Mexico are in a polite diplomatic battle over the value of the marketplace for illegal drugs in the U.S. and the size of the Mexican cartels' slice of the pie. U.S. law enforcement, eager for more dollars for their efforts, optimistically values the market in the tens of billions of dollars, while the Mexican government, anxious not to be perceived by the rest of the world as an economy wholly dependent on profits from illicit markets, tends to be much more conservative.

At the Border Security Conference, hosted annually by the University of Texas at El Paso, in August 2010, Alejandro Hope Pinsón—Director of International Affairs, Center for Research and National Security (CISEN), Government of Mexico—said that the trafficking of illegal drugs represents a "high value, low volume activity." The government of Mexico estimates that illegal drugs account for about 8 percent of the total value of the U.S./Mexico trade while only accounting for about 0.004 percent of the total volume of U.S./Mexico trade. He asserted that all drugs coming from Mexico to the United States annually would fit into 60 trucks, a remarkable figure when you consider that 15,000 trucks cross the border every day just in Laredo, Texas.

"The production estimates of marijuana in Mexico made by the U.S. intelligence community would imply that 215 million Americans (which are about 70 percent of all Americans) smoke 200 joints of Mexican marijuana every single year. Just Mexican marijuana. Which of course, we don't think that is the case."

Mr. Hope Pinsón says that the government of Mexico estimates that the cartels make between $3 billion and $9 billion from wholesale drug exports. "We tend to believe this is 90 to 95 percent of their income and that some of the claims that their income is in the tens of billions of dollars are just wrong. Plain wrong."

The Mexican government estimates that the cartels take of the marijuana market in the U.S. is between $750 million to $3 billion. For cocaine, they estimate between $1.65 billion to $4.8 billion. Heroin brings in between $300 to $700 million and methamphetamine between $160 million to $480 million.[23]

The United States government is much more bullish about the revenues made by Mexican drug cartels, estimating that Mexican cartels bring home between $15 billion to $30 billion annually from illicit drug sales.[24] At one point, the White House Office of National Drug Control Policy estimated that more than 60 percent of the cartels' revenue—$8.6 billion out of $13.8 billion in 2006—came from U.S. marijuana sales. They retracted those estimates in 2010,[25] but continue to assert that marijuana is the top revenue generator for Mexican drug cartels.[26]

Just looking at retail value or gross revenue estimates, it's easy to assume cocaine is the most profitable business center in the Mexican cartel's portfolio. But gross revenues don't give a full picture of profitability. A review of costs, market demand and risk is important to assessing which drug brings the most value to the cartels.

Marijuana has the largest customer base with the most stable demand and steady prices. Cocaine prices, costs and demand are more volatile. Marijuana is the cheapest drug to cultivate and produce while cocaine goes through an expensive manufacturing process. The cartels pay about $23 to buy a pound of marijuana from a farmer in Mexico. It costs the cartels about $4,000 to buy a pound of cocaine from the Colombians to import to the U.S. Cocaine also has a longer supply chain through more international borders than marijuana, increasing the risks of seizures.

While cocaine has a higher retail value than marijuana, the markup for marijuana is higher. For example, a cartel can buy a pound of marijuana for $23 in Mexico and sell it for $550 a pound in Chicago, or 23 times the initial investment. They could buy a pound of cocaine for $4,000 from the Colombians and sell it for $32,000 a pound in Chicago, only eight times the initial investment.

The Mexican cartels own the value of marijuana from farm to market. The cocaine market is not vertically integrated. The Mexican cartels buy cocaine from producers in the Andes region, decreasing their share of the markup in comparison to marijuana.

★

Estimating the size and value of the illegal drug market is a black art muddied with lots of grasping assumptions like what percentage of the total market is seized or eradicated or how truthful people are when they are surveyed about their illicit drug activity. Another way to consider the enormity and profitability of the illegal drug market value is to consider how much the industry can sustain in losses and not go out of business.

Before 2008, public officials in both the U.S. and Mexico were still able to shrug off the violence as a momentary chaos that would end shortly as soon as one cartel or another established control of the plaza. Calderón's war against the cartels was in full swing. The U.S. was beginning to step up with more resources, not just in Mexico; they were also implementing more southbound checks for guns and weapons and more aggressive intelligence strategies to blunt gun smuggling and bulk cash smuggling into Mexico.

In 2008, illegal drug markets serving the U.S. demand lost approximately 22,000 metric tons of marijuana. The marijuana was seized by law enforcement in the United States and Mexico, or it was eradicated.[27]

Two approaches to developing estimates of the market size of marijuana paint wildly different views of the size of the marijuana market. Average demand-side estimates for marijuana are about 3,000 metric tons consumed annually by Americans, while supply-side estimates, which are less reliable, run as high as 24,000 metric tons. Regardless of what you believe to be the most reliable estimate—3,000 metric tons or 24,000 metric tons—it is astounding that drug traffickers are still able to remain profitable after losing 22,200 metric tons of product. Losses of that magnitude are almost eight times the size of average demand-side estimates of market size, and roughly equal to the market calculated by the highest supply-side estimates. There are not many legal industries that can lose between 50 to 90 percent of their product and still think it is a worthwhile investment.

Beyond marijuana losses, there were other documented business losses in 2008 as well:

★ 358 metric tons of cocaine seized or eradicated (the average estimate for the cocaine market is 300 metric tons purchased annually);

★ 75.17 metric tons of heroin seized or eradicated (the average estimate for the heroin market is 22 metric tons purchased annually);

★ 6.65 metric tons of methamphetamine (the average estimate for the methamphetamine market is 22 metric tons purchased annually);

- ★ $1 billion in bulk cash seizures in the United States and Mexico;
- ★ 7 senior level managers of the cartels arrested by the Mexican government in 2008, including Alfredo Beltran Leyva and Jesus "El Rey" Zambada Garcia of the Sinaloa cartel; Reynosa plaza boss Antonio "El Amarillo" Gallarza Coronado and enforcer Jaime "El Hummer" Gonzalez Duran of the Gulf cartel; Eduardo Arellano Felix and Luis Romero, principals of the Arellano Felix organization; and Colombian trafficker Pedro Antonio Ramirez;
- ★ 5,153 people killed in Mexico as part of the drug violence (presumably some of those killed worked in the drug trade but because only 3 percent of murders are investigated, it is difficult to know how many were business associates and how many were innocent bystanders);
- ★ 28,650 people arrested on drug-related charges in Mexico (the same presumption in the previous bullet applies here);
- ★ more than 20,000 firearms seized, half of them assault rifles;
- ★ 2,600,000 rounds of ammunition seized in Mexico;
- ★ and, other notable business losses included drug labs being destroyed and massive seizures of vehicles, grenades and explosive devices.

Beyond the losses in inventory and the turnover in personnel, the illegal drug industry also has huge resources from both Mexico and the United States mounted against their efforts to move illegal drugs to the United States market. In an attempt to curtail an illegal drug market, estimated to be valued at between $63 billion and $81 billion, the United States has marshaled $49 billion in federal, state and local dollars[28] and Mexico has increased their annual security funding from $5 billion to $10 billion since Calderón took office.[29]

CHAPTER 4
MARKET FORCES

In December of 2007, Jesse Aranda, José Luis (Gordo) Terrazas and Paul Quaintance met at Paul's ranch in Chaparral, New Mexico. Chaparral is a small rural town just past northeast El Paso. It's known for dirt roads and mobile homes set on large parcels of barren land and for residents who like to be left alone to do their own thing.

Jesse, Gordo and Paul met to talk business and to inspect 400 pounds of pot.

Jesse was an independent broker who found buyers for illegal drugs in U.S. markets. He had a buyer for 1,600 pounds of pot in Atlanta.

Gordo was an El Paso broker—he organized the logistics for warehousing and transporting drug shipments coming from Juárez through El Paso to U.S. markets. He priced his services according to the destination, examining the risk of getting the product to market and the value of the product in the market. He might charge $80 a pound for his services depending on where the load was headed, keeping $10 a pound for himself and paying the rest for transportation services.

Paul handled warehousing and transportation for Gordo. He stored the marijuana at his ranch, cleaned and wrapped it and coordinated the transportation to its destination. He had a truck and two drivers.

The pot was supplied by the Sinaloan cartel, who had it shipped to El Paso through two Juárez brokers who worked directly for the Sinaloan cartel.

Unlike Mexican brokers, brokers in the United States don't have to be aligned with any particular cartel, but the cartels make it a point to make sure that the brokers know who is supplying the product. This particular deal was detailed in a federal court case against a high-ranking member of the Sinaloan cartel in Juárez. Gordo explained in the court case that the cartels want you to know who supplied the load "so you'll be respectful, so you will pay soon...It's like they intimidate people so people will pay them quickly." If you don't pay on time, "they'll pick you up and take you away."

The night that Jesse, Gordo and Paul met in Chaparral, they inspected the 400 pounds. Jesse, representing the Atlanta buyer, examined the color and the smell. He made sure there were no seeds. He made sure that it was loose and not compressed. After his examination, he agreed that it looked good and agreed to buy 1,600 pounds. They agreed on a price of $525 a pound, or $840,000 for the 1,600 pound load.

The marijuana was shipped to Atlanta right away. Gordo, as the El Paso broker, was responsible for tracking the load to make sure that it arrived in Atlanta and was delivered to Jesse, the Atlanta broker. Jesse drove to Atlanta separately to meet the load and deliver it to his buyer. Jesse made his cut of the transaction by increasing the price, "From $25 to $50 a pound. It all depends on the client." He planned to sell this load for $650 a pound, or $1,040,000. He was buying the load for $840,000, so he stood to make $200,000 from the sale in Atlanta, minus his expenses.

When the marijuana arrived in Atlanta, Jesse and the buyer met the load and paid the drivers $80,000. The drivers kept $40,000 for themselves and returned the other half to Paul.

What should have happened next was that the Atlanta buyer would pay Jesse $1,040,000. Jesse would take his cut and send $840,000 back down to El Paso. The couriers who brought the money back to El Paso would take 2 to 3 percent. Normally, payment was expected in 10 days to two weeks from the date of delivery.

But that is not what happened.

Jesse and his Atlanta buyer did not immediately inspect the marijuana when it was delivered. As a precaution against being caught, they waited for a couple days before they inspected it. When they inspected it, the buyer told Jesse that only one part of the load was good. The other part wasn't good. It was seedy, brown and old. He didn't want to pay for the bad stuff.

The buyer sold the good marijuana right away, but insisted on returning the bad stuff. He didn't pay Jesse for any of it. Jesse called Gordo, the El Paso broker, to tell him that a portion of the marijuana was not good and that the buyer wanted to return the bad marijuana. Word got sent back up to Jesse through Gordo that the cartels had a no-return policy regardless of quality, and he was on the hook for the money regardless of whether or not he was paid.

When the payment for the load didn't arrive back in Juárez in two weeks, the Juárez broker started hassling Gordo, the El Paso broker, for the money. Gordo was given a choice: either pay up or bring Jesse, the Atlanta broker, back down from Atlanta to account for the money. If he didn't do either of these things, they would pick him up.

Normally, information about other players in a transaction is limited. Losing a load changes things. When the Juárez brokers started hassling Gordo, he in return started hassling Jesse in Atlanta. Before the transaction went sour, the Juárez brokers didn't know Jesse and didn't know how to get in touch with him. Under pressure from the Juárez brokers, Gordo gave up Jesse's phone number. "Because if I didn't give the number…I would get in trouble. And I didn't want to get picked up." He feared that the Sinaloan cartel would kill him if he didn't pay up.

The Juárez brokers working directly for the Sinaloan cartel started threatening Jesse. Jesse said that one of them "told me that he knows where my wife was driving, where she lives. He told me the license plates on her car and everything."

When the Juárez brokers were not able to get the money for the load, the cartel leadership got involved. Jesse knew it was really bad when he started getting calls directly from two of the main guys of the Sinolaon cartel in Juárez, El Fer and El Mayito.

Jesse and Gordo were desperate. They even considered drugging the Atlanta buyer with morphine and bringing him back to the border. Knowing his life was at risk, the Atlanta buyer went into hiding. Jesse hired a private investigator to track the buyer down. The private investigator got spooked and wouldn't handle the job. He called later and said that he knew a bounty hunter who would take the job. The bounty hunter turned out to be an undercover DEA agent.

And that's how Jesse and El Gordo ended up testifying in a federal drug smuggling case.

★

Jesse and Gordo noted that things started to change in late 2007 and 2008 in Juárez. Both said that the amount of time that the cartels were giving the brokers to send back the money was shortening. The demand for money was becoming insistent, and the tactics used to retrieve the money were becoming more extreme and more violent.[30]

There was a supply issue. And there was a supplier issue. And the brokers were feeling the pinch.

CHAPTER 5
SUPPLY

Starting in the early 1990s, the Juárez cartel owned the Juárez plaza and therefore they regulated access to the plaza. Cocaine was always tightly controlled by the Juárez cartel. No one else but the Juárez cartel could traffic cocaine through the Juárez corridor. If you violated these rules, you were eliminated. "There was a case of someone from Guadalajara who started shipping cocaine by bus to Juárez. He was caught. He was tortured and hung and his body thrown by the Galgódromo in Juárez."[31]

The rules for trafficking in marijuana were different than for cocaine in Juárez when Amado Carrillo Fuentes ruled the plaza in the 1990s. Unlike cocaine, other cartels and even independent *marijuaneros* (entrepreneurs who grew and sold marijuana) could move marijuana through the plaza as long as they paid a *derecho de piso* or fee to the Juárez cartel for the rights of access. Because of this rule, there were many independent entrepreneurs and farmers trafficking marijuana through Juárez.[32]

One of the business decisions that Vicente made when he took control of the plaza after his brother's death was that the Juárez cartel would control the market for marijuana, the same as they did for cocaine. Because they owned the plaza, they could impose such a monopoly. The monopoly allowed them to become more profitable in the marijuana trade because they went from charging a fee for marijuana moving through the plaza to owning the marijuana market from farm to market. Other cartels and the independent *marijuaneros* could no longer move marijuana through the plaza.[33]

In order to impose the monopoly on marijuana, the Juárez cartel was under pressure to produce as much marijuana as was previously produced and transited through Juárez by other cartels and *marijuaneros*. Their inability to do this put control of the plaza at risk.

★

Prosecutor: And back in 2008, was—were things changing in the drug business here in El Paso?

Gordo: Yes, sir.

Prosecutor: And why were these changes taking place?

Gordo: Because there was a big war in Mexico between the cartels, and marijuana went up in price.

Prosecutor: And who were the warring cartels?

Gordo: The Sinaloa and the Juárez.

Prosecutor: And why was it that this war was taking place?

Gordo: They were fighting for the plaza, for the location in Juárez.

Prosecutor: Now, you said something about the price of marijuana during the war. What was happening to the price of marijuana?

Gordo: It went up, because there wasn't much marijuana here in El Paso. And, also, because they were having trouble there in Mexico.

Prosecutor: And was marijuana harder to get?

Gordo: Yes, sir.

Prosecutor: And was something happening with regards to the cartels and the cartels wanting payment for the marijuana?

Gordo: Yes, sir.

Prosecutor: And what was happening?

Gordo: That, at that time, they were having difficulty with the marijuana, and they wanted quick payment.

Prosecutor: And when people weren't getting quick payment, the cartels weren't getting quick payment, what was happening?

Gordo: They would put a lot of pressure on those who owed.

Prosecutor: What sort of pressure would they put on these people?

Gordo: To scare them, to threaten them, to tell you that if you didn't pay up, they would pick you up.[34]

★

Sergio Saucedo, a marijuana broker for the Juárez cartel, refused to go to Juárez to explain how he lost a load that he got on credit. Sergio lived in Horizon City, just east of El Paso. On September 3, 2009, Sergio and his family came home to find three armed men in their house. The men ducttaped the parents' hands, took the kids upstairs and kidnapped Sergio. Sergio was held hostage for a week in Juárez to try to exact a payment for the load. When he couldn't pay up, he was murdered. His hands were chopped off and laid across his chest, a warning to others about the dangers of not paying on time.

Gordo's testimony on the tightening supply of marijuana and attendant increase in price through the Juárez corridor is validated by DEA figures on El Paso wholesale prices and by seizure data from the National Seizure Center. In 2007, the wholesale price of marijuana in El Paso was between $200 and $225 a pound. The price in 2010 increased to $280 to $300 a pound.[35]

Seizure data, a good indicator of market activity, also backs up Gordo's testimony. Marijuana seizures were fairly steady through El Paso and Doña Ana County through 2007, the two counties that share a border with Juárez, indicating a fairly steady flow of marijuana through the corridor. Then the market tightened, expanded and rapidly tightened again. Between 2007 and 2010, marijuana seizures decreased by a dramatic 69 percent. As supply tightens, the number of people murdered in Juárez soars. (See graph on page 55)

Oddly enough while supply for marijuana was tightening in Juárez, the available supply for export from the rest of Mexico was increasing dramatically. When President Calderón decided to take the war against the cartels to the cities, he diverted the Mexican army from their traditional eradication efforts to urban warfare. The result of that strategy was that less and less pot was being destroyed and so more and more was available for cultivation and export into the U.S. (See graph on page 56)

Mexico was routinely eradicating 30,000 or more hectares of marijuana every year until Calderón declared war on the cartels in 2006. In 2010, Mexico only eradicated 17,211 hectares, down 43 percent from

MARIJUANA SEIZURES IN EL PASO & DOÑA ANA COUNTY COMPARED TO HOMICIDES IN JUÁREZ

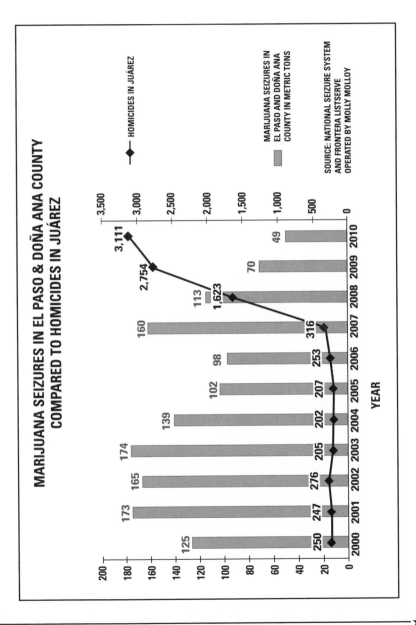

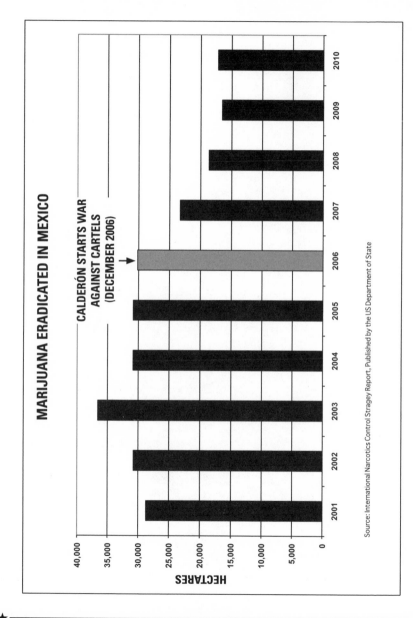

MARIJUANA ERADICATED IN MEXICO

CALDERÓN STARTS WAR
AGAINST CARTELS
(DECEMBER 2006)

HECTARES

40,000
35,000
30,000
25,000
20,000
15,000
10,000
5,000
0

2001 2002 2003 2004 2005 2006 2007 2008 2009 2010

Source: International Narcotics Control Stragey Report, Published by the US Department of State

2006. As less marijuana was eradicated, more was cultivated and more made its way north to U.S. markets. The U.S. government estimates that the cultivation of marijuana has increased from 5,600 hectares in 2005 to almost 17,500 hectares in 2009.[36]

U.S. law enforcement also saw this trend through a sharp uptick in seizures of pot at the U.S./Mexico border. (See graph on page 58)

Other border communities in Mexico picked up the slack when Juárez lost market share and when Mexico increased its marijuana crop yield. At the same time that Juárez was losing prominence in supplying marijuana to the U.S. market, South Texas and Arizona counties began to see significant spikes in marijuana seizures at and between ports of entry. Mexican cartels increased their imports into the U.S. market for marijuana—undercutting domestic producers on price and increasing their market share—but less was coming through Juárez.

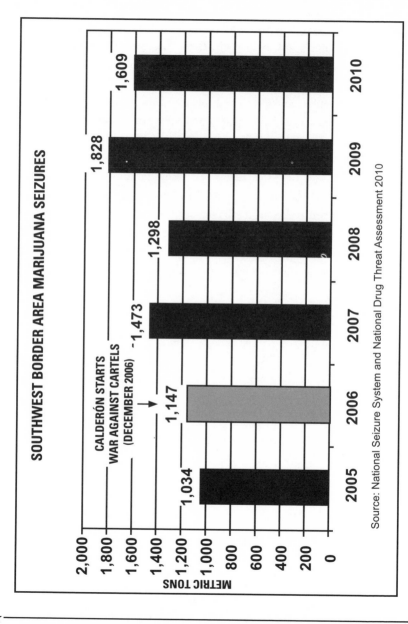

SOUTHWEST BORDER AREA MARIJUANA SEIZURES

CALDERÓN STARTS
WAR AGAINST CARTELS
(DECEMBER 2006)

Year	Metric Tons
2005	1,034
2006	1,147
2007	1,473
2008	1,298
2009	1,828
2010	1,609

METRIC TONS

Source: National Seizure System and National Drug Threat Assessment 2010

CHAPTER 6
MARKET SHARE

Prosecutor: Okay. And who did *Árabe* later tell you he got the marijuana from?

Jesse Aranda: From *El Mayito*.

Prosecutor: *El Mayito*? And who is *Mayito*?

Jesse Aranda: That's a well-known person in Mexico, in Juárez.

Prosecutor: Okay. And what does he do?

Jesse Aranda: Drug dealer.

Prosecutor: Okay. And if you know, is he associated with a certain group or cartel?

Jesse Aranda: Yes, sir.

Prosecutor: Which group is he associated with?

Jesse Aranda: *El Chapo* Guzmán. [Sinaloan cartel]

Prosecutor: Now, have you ever met this *Mayito*?

Jesse Aranda: Yes, sir.

Prosecutor: And where did you meet him?

Jesse Aranda: In Juárez.

Prosecutor: And about when was it that you met him?

Jesse Aranda: About three years before this.

Prosecutor: Back in 2005?

Jesse Aranda: 2005, 2006, around there.

Prosecutor: And who introduced you to *Mayito*?

Jesse Aranda: Mr. Oscar Martinez.

Prosecutor: And who is this Oscar Martinez?

Jesse Aranda: He was his partner, I guess, or—he was something—in the same category as him.

Prosecutor: Okay.

Jesse Aranda: I used to work for him.

Prosecutor: Okay. You used to work for him?

Jesse Aranda: Yes, sir.

Prosecutor: And did—this Oscar Martinez, did he work for anyone?

Jesse Aranda: He was working for *La Línea* at the moment.

Prosecutor: For *La Línea*. And *La Línea* is—what also is *La Línea* known as?

Jesse Aranda: As the other cartel against *El Chapo*.

Prosecutor: Against *Chapo*. Which region in Mexico are they—this *La Línea* based out of?

Jesse Aranda: Juárez.

Prosecutor: And do you know who the ultimate leader of the—of this *La Línea*, or the Juárez cartel is?

Jesse Aranda: Yes, sir.

Prosecutor: Who is that?

Jesse Aranda: Vicente Carrillo.

Prosecutor: Now, was there a time when Oscar Martinez switched allegiances from the Juárez cartel?

Jesse Aranda: Yes, sir.

Prosecutor: And who did he switch to?

Jesse Aranda: He—I don't know if he switched, but he is the one that opened the door for *Chapo* to come in through Juárez.

Prosecutor: Okay. And how do you know this?

Jesse Aranda: By—he talked to me. He told me about it, and he said he was going to change because his work was more marijuana than cocaine, and *Chapo* and *Mayito* were the ones that were producing the more marijuana.

Prosecutor: Okay. And was this Oscar Martinez going to help—was Oscar Martinez going to come in and open up the corridor for who?

Jesse Aranda: For *Mayito*.[37]

CHAPTER 7
MARKET DISRUPTION

On June 17, 1971, President Richard Nixon declared war on drugs. "Public enemy No. 1 in the United States is drug abuse. In order to fight and defeat this enemy, it is necessary to wage a new, all-out offensive." At his press conference, Nixon laid out a plan to build a central agency—the Special Action Office of Drug Abuse Prevention—to coordinate the federal response to drug abuse. He asked for an additional $371 million from Congress to "conquer drug abuse in America." His funding request included new dollars for the treatment, prevention, education, eradication and stepped up enforcement of existing drug trafficking laws.

"When traffic in narcotics is no longer profitable, then that traffic will cease. Increased enforcement and vigorous application of the fullest penalties provided by law are two of the steps in rendering narcotics trade unprofitable."[38] Nixon ended his declaration detailing the federal government's new role in ending drug abuse by stating, "The final issue is not whether we will conquer drug abuse, but how soon."[39]

Our federal drug-war budget has ballooned from Nixon's $371 million request to $15.6 billion dollars within 40 years. State and local governments spend an additional $33.1 billion annually towards drug enforcement.

In addition to the new resources and federal resolve to end drug abuse announced by President Nixon in 1971, any time a drug epidemic panicked the public, federal officials responded by increasing their firepower in the war against drugs.

The most recent escalation in the war has focused south of the border. First, there was Merida funding, $1.4 billion in aid to go to Mexico and Central America over a period of three years to support efforts to curb drug trafficking.

As President Calderón's war began to boil and rage in Mexico and U.S. politicians—conflating the economic battle over drugs with the emotional issues of border security and immigration—began railing against the possibility of "spillover," the U.S. ramped up its efforts to disrupt the Mexican cartels with new resources focused on the border. Secretary of Homeland Security Janet Napolitano described the need for this new build-up of resources at the 2010 Border Security Conference sponsored by Congressman Silvestre Reyes and hosted by the University of Texas at El Paso: "…we have a unique opportunity now with Mexico to really break up these cartels, and shame on us if we don't take full advantage of that opportunity and go through the window together."

At the conference, Napolitano announced that $75 million in Operation Stonegarden funding was headed to the border to improve "law enforcement preparedness and operational readiness" in case of the much-feared spillover. "So for you law enforcement folks in the audience, what this means is that in the past eight months, almost 85 percent of all Stonegarden money nationally has gone right here to the Southwest border. You can clap for that. That's okay."

There was more for law enforcement to clap for. "In the past six months, we have added hundreds of agents and deployed additional technology to the border. We've doubled the number of agents that U.S. Immigration and Customs Enforcement has assigned to the border enforcement security teams, which include American, Mexican, state, local, [and] tribal law enforcement agents, working together to crack down on smuggling. We have tripled the number of Department of Homeland

Security [DHS] intelligence analysts working on the Southwest border. We have doubled the number of DHS agents collaborating on looking for and apprehending violent criminal aliens; we have, as you know, ramped up southbound inspections to search for illegal weapons and cash, adding mobile X-ray machines, license plate readers, more Border Patrol agents, and K-9 detection teams to that effort. For the first time we have begun inspecting all southbound rail shipments into Mexico."

Her colleagues from other federal agencies who spoke at the Border Security conference also breathlessly announced millions of new dollars and other doubling and tripling of resources focused on the fight against the Mexican cartels.

In a time of increasing debate over almost every penny spent by the feds—a debate that almost shut down the government in 2011—it seems strange that law enforcement programs, unlike treatment and prevention programs, are almost never held up to scrutiny. Public officials demand accountability and constant assessments of prevention and treatment programs. They want to know that investment in those strategies will pay off. Do they work? As a result, there are exhaustive studies looking at whether prevention programs keep kids from lighting up that first joint and whether treatment programs help drug addicts come clean and stay clean.

It is rare for public officials to demand that same accountability from law enforcement efforts to "conquer drug abuse." As a result, there are few studies examining what the impact of law enforcement efforts have been on American's access to and use of illegal drugs. When elected officials do raise concerns about the success of law enforcement efforts, they are usually headed off at the pass with moral absolutes like, "We have to keep drugs out of the hands of children," that assume that we are doing just that with current drug policy.

While there are few studies on the effectiveness of the drug war, we do have information about where we were when we started and where we are now.

Law enforcement efforts to disrupt illegal drug markets are focused along the whole supply chain, from farm to market. Law enforcement strategies include eradicating poppies, opium and marijuana, closing down production labs, seizing product on its way to market with increasing efforts and resources focused on ports of entry and routes leaving border cities, arresting people who participate in the drug trade (traffickers, dealers, buyers) and seizing money and assets amassed by these same people.

The hope behind supply-side law enforcement efforts (eradication and seizures) is that if law enforcement seizes enough product, it will limit supplies of that product in American markets. Limited supplies will then force drug dealers to increase their price or decrease the purity or do both to continue to feed the demand with a more limited supply. The thought behind the strategy is that a higher price and a less powerful high will reduce the customer base and curb enthusiasm for new participants to enter the marketplace.

In his comments at the 2010 Border Security Conference, U.S. Drug Czar Gil Kerlikowske highlighted the theory behind law enforcement strategies aimed at limiting supplies of illegal drugs in American markets by making these remarks about the possibility of legalizing marijuana: "One more reason why the U.S. is absolutely opposed to the legalization of any drug: legalizing drugs makes them cheaper, makes them more accessible, and therefore makes them more widely abused." Based on this logic about legalization, we should then assume that prohibition and 40 years of the drug war eradication and seizures has made illegal drugs more expensive, less accessible and less widely abused.

The reality is just the opposite. Cocaine's market history most obviously undermines the theories perpetuated by U.S. policymakers who support prohibition. The U.S. really ratcheted up the war against cocaine and the Colombian cartels in the 1980s. These efforts were largely successful in shutting down the Florida peninsula as a trade route for cocaine into the United States. These efforts significantly diminished the power of Colombian cartels in the American marketplace for illegal drugs.

According to the logic behind law enforcement supply-side strategies, cocaine should now be incredibly expensive since the most logical and most efficient transportation corridor into the U.S. market has been shut down, weakening the Colombian cartels as a result. In fact, between 1981 and 2003, powder cocaine prices declined cumulatively by roughly 80 percent. They decreased again between 2004 and 2007 from $145 per gram to $125 per gram.[40] There have been increases in the price of cocaine from 2007 to 2011 that law enforcement in the U.S. and Mexico point to as a sign of their winning the battle against Mexican cartels, but these prices are nowhere close to the all-time high in the early 80s. Not only is cocaine much less expensive since its heyday in the 1980s, it is also purer.

According to the drug czar, making illegal drugs more affordable should then increase availability and therefore lead to more abuse. In fact, cocaine availability was very high and its use was at its highest when the drug was the most expensive in the early 1980s. In 1977, 33 percent of high school seniors said that cocaine was fairly easy or very easy to get. That number rose to 48 percent in 1980 when prices were at their highest, holding steady until 1989 when it rose to 59 percent. It has now dropped down again to pre-1980s availability.[41]

Despite law enforcement's best efforts, the price of cocaine has dropped precipitously since 1981. When cocaine was most expensive in 1981, about 12 percent of high school seniors reported using it. After an 80 percent dip in price to 2003, only 5 percent of high school seniors reported using cocaine.[42] Making cocaine more affordable did not increase abuse.

Marijuana is harder to use as an example for how law enforcement efforts might shift changes in price and availability because the supply, demand and retail price is steady and constant and doesn't spike and wane like other, harder drugs. Pricing differences in marijuana are normally attributable to quality and potency, rather than shifts in use or law enforcement efforts. Its potency is at the highest levels ever recorded as producers respond to consumer demand for a premium product.[43]

The fact is that drug use and abuse seem to follow patterns outside the control and influence of law enforcement efforts to disrupt markets. They might get the bad guys. They might stop a ton of marijuana from making it across from Mexico. But that hasn't influenced whether or not a 15-year-old in Chicago decides to light her first joint.

In a review of public policies that might reduce demand for drugs in the United States in a significant enough way to reduce violence in Mexico in the next five years, Peter Reuter—one of the leading academics in drug war policy—determined, "Enforcement which aims to raise prices and make drugs less available has simply not shown a capacity to do that on more than an episodic basis."[44]

★

In addition to the drug war having no appreciable impact on curbing drug access and drug abuse, the market for illegal drugs in the United States has created a sizable underground economy that has killed over 45,000 people in Mexico as part of the price of doing business. And the horrors aren't confined to Mexico; daily shootings in American inner cities are largely attributable to drug turf disputes. U.S. efforts to disrupt the flows of illegal products into the United States have created business organizations that are deadly, nimble, innovative and complex. They have far outpaced law enforcement in technological advances aimed at moving illegal drugs through a dizzying array of obstacles and law enforcement escalation.

One drug trafficking organization may topple, its leadership wiped out or captured, only to be replaced by other more resilient, more sophisticated organizations who more tightly control and regulate the market. A corridor may be shut down by aggressive law enforcement efforts, making it unprofitable to move illegal drugs through that area. That corridor will be replaced by others. Law enforcement will shut down the ability to move product to the U.S. on planes, and the next thing you know, the drug trafficking organizations have deployed semi-submersible submarines, built transport tunnels between Mexico and the U.S., or are catapulting marijuana over the billion-dollar fence built on the U.S./Mexico border.

What doesn't change each time law enforcement strikes a blow against a drug trafficking organization is the demand for drugs and the huge profits associated with meeting that demand. This phenomenon is referred to as the balloon effect or the many headed hydra or Whac-A-Mole, depending on your propensity for wonky, Greek or popular culture references. The U.S. and its drug war allies can wipe out an organization or a bad guy or a street dealer or a straw purchaser of firearms or a money man or a corrupt customs agent. They do it all day long and they send out press releases letting us know what happened.

But what the U.S. and its drug war allies can't do using current drug war strategies is to wipe out the huge profits to be made in the market for illegal drugs. In fact, it is these very efforts by law enforcement that have made selling illegal drugs so profitable.

Like any successful entrepreneurs, drug cartels are constantly re-shaping their product and their business model to respond to market shifts and to increase their profitability. The Colombian cartels that were the focus of so much of the United States' attention and energy in the 1980s and early 1990s only trafficked in cocaine. When their trafficking corridors were shut down by law enforcement efforts, the Colombian cartels began to depend more and more on Mexican cartels to move their cocaine to market. In the late 1980s and 1990s, Mexican cartels moved about 50 percent of Columbian cocaine through Mexico to the U.S. Today, the Mexican cartels are responsible for moving 90 percent of the cocaine through Mexico.

As the demand for cocaine in the United States has diminished over the last decade, so has the Colombian's power in the market. The Mexican cartels in power today picked up the slack, evolving into more complex organizations that move a diverse portfolio of drugs to market. Colombian cartels only manufactured and sold cocaine. Mexican cartels today grow and sell marijuana. They grow, manufacture and sell heroin. They manufacture and sell methamphetamines. They buy and sell cocaine. As one market for illegal drugs shrinks, the Mexican cartels respond by growing other business centers or by increasing their profitability within a shrinking market.

Bombarded with daily reports detailing the shocking violence of the drug wars, drug enforcement agents in the U.S. and Mexico appear oddly optimistic and determined to stay the course. At least in their public remarks. "The reason you see the escalation in violence is because U.S. and Mexican law enforcement are winning," said Garrison Courtney of the DEA. "You are going to see the drug traffickers push back because we are breaking their back. It's reasonable to assume they are going to try to fight to stay relevant."[45]

These remarks were later echoed by Michele Leonhart, head of the Drug Enforcement Administration. In the face of rising numbers of murdered children and civilians in Mexico, she said, "It may seem contradictory, but the unfortunate level of violence is a sign of success in the fight against drugs."[46]

★

Yet the contradiction is hard to shake. More than 40,000 dead in Mexico just doesn't seem like success. But this violent response to a war on drugs isn't unique to Mexico or to our times. We have faced a similar disconnect between the aims and realities of law enforcement—during a previous attempt to prohibit something for which we also had an insatiable appetite: alcohol—that produced one of the most violent criminal eras in U.S. history.

CHAPTER 8
GOVERNING OUR DESIRES– ALCOHOL AND MARIJUANA

El Paso, Texas was one of the first municipalities to ban marijuana, influenced to a large degree by a sensational New Year's Day murder in 1913. The culprit was presumed to be intoxicated by marijuana, a drug that was then thought to have "a more dreadful effect than opium, creating in its victim hallucinations which frequently result in violent crimes."[47]

Marijuana was closely identified with Mexico and Mexicans. The *El Paso Herald* article described marijuana as "that native Mexican herb which causes the smoker to crave murder," making clear the origin and effect of what, to many U.S. citizens, was a previously unknown substance.

"Crazed by continual use of the drug," the newspaper report continues, "an unidentified Mexican killed a policeman, wounded another, stabbed two horses and pursued an El Paso woman and her escort, brandishing a huge knife in the air."

The ordinance banning marijuana was some time in coming, and despite the sensational reaction to the murder, El Paso pharmacies continued to sell the drug. Ironically, there was little demand for it until it was made illegal. A longtime El Paso pharmacist recounted that

> Up until 1921, it was not illegal to sell marijuana. But neither was there any big demand for it. We kept it in 1-ounce packages which sold for 25 cents. Every now and then a man in work clothes would walk in and buy a quarter's worth to take home and smoke just for relaxation.
>
> Since 1921, when the plant and its use as a drug was prohibited from sale, the demand has been growing.[48]

Despite the fact that few used it, that there had been little to no scientific review of the claims raised by the newspaper, the *El Paso Herald* had its readers believe that marijuana was a dangerous drug, and Mexicans on marijuana were a threat to public health and safety. It's no wonder the El Paso City Council moved to criminalize the drug soon after.

★

El Paso was not unique in rushing to ban a substance based on fear or best intentions. For millennia we have incorporated a range of drugs into our habits and ceremonies to help us deal with daily life or even transcend it: the wine that unwinds, the caffeine that powers, the tobacco that calms and the marijuana that relieves. And for almost as long, we've struggled to determine how these drugs best fit into our lives and our communities.

At their chemical and biological heart they are poisons, evolved to disorient and sicken the curious animals who might try to dine on their host plants. And yet some animals have persisted in consuming, and in the case of humans, ultimately cultivating, these psychoactive substances for their power to stimulate, hallucinate and relax.[49]

Through a quirk of evolution and chemistry, the molecules in the toxic alkaloids that enter our bloodstream and pass the blood-brain barrier when we drink a beer or smoke a joint are able to fool our natural defenses against poisons and instead produce signals in our brain that equate to euphoria and relief, mimicking neurotransmitters in the brain's reward and pain-control centers.[50]

Two of these intoxicants (Latin for "poison") have held special sway over much of human history. Alcohol and marijuana are central to much of our culture, our way of life and our laws.

ALCOHOL

Pure alcohol, or ethanol, is a colorless, flammable and volatile liquid that inhibits the functions of the central nervous system. A drink or two, and one enjoys feelings of euphoria and finds that his inhibitions are lowered. A few more, and motor functions are impaired and brain activity is slowed, words are slurred and sleep beckons. Too much, and it is fatal. The effects linger: after a good drunk, nausea, lethargy and a heightened sensitivity to loud noises can persist for days.[51]

When man began to cultivate alcohol for his enjoyment is unknown, but the consensus is that sometime between 10,000 B.C. to 8000 B.C, he took the step from enjoying alcohol when he came upon it naturally, for example the residue produced by decaying fruits and plants, to actually cultivating the process and storing its product.

It is thought that wine was developed sometime between 6000 B.C and 4000 B.C in the vicinity of modern day Armenia and Iran.[52] It has been a dominant psychoactive fixture for much of human development since then, with commercial vineyards established as early as 1500 B.C.

It is also a cornerstone of Western culture and is a central component of Judeo-Christian religious texts and practices. It's mentioned throughout the Bible, from Noah's post-flood bender to the story of Jesus turning water into wine. It is a central part of the Catholic mass, where it is believed that wine is transubstantiated into the blood of Christ.

The first Puritan ships to reach America delivered over 10,000 gallons of wine.[53] Today over 784 million gallons are consumed each year in the United States alone.[54]

Add to wine all of the other alcoholic beverages found throughout the world, and it becomes clear how fundamental a part of life it is for humanity. All told, it is enjoyed by an estimated 2 billion people worldwide.

Besides the short-term benefits and drawbacks outlined above, alcohol has serious implications for long-term health. On the positive side, moderate use may reduce the risk of developing heart disease or of dying of a heart attack. It may also reduce the risk of some kinds of strokes. Its drawbacks are numerous, and include addiction, cirrhosis of the liver, cancers and injuries. The dangers of drunk driving and violence—because these actions impact the community, not just the drinker—are perhaps even more serious. These negative impacts of alcohol use result in approximately 2.5 million deaths each year.

★

While alcohol consumption has been central to American life dating from the first European settlers, so has the effort to restrict or prohibit its use. Diverse interest groups, from suffragettes, to anti-Catholic and anti-immigrant Protestants, from well-meaning teetotalers to Southern racists, pushed the prohibition agenda, their efforts coming to a head in the early 20th century.

In an ugly foreshadowing of the language that would be used to criminalize marijuana by tying it to Mexican immigrants, some of the most powerful rhetoric used in the alcohol prohibition movement played upon white fears of African Americans.

In a speech on the floor of the House of Representatives in 1917 (the year that the 18th amendment language was adopted by the U.S. Congress)

Congressmen John Tillman of Arkansas informed his colleagues that liquor "increases the menace of [the black man's] presence." However, his comments were not just reflective of Southern racists. Frances Willard, a leading voice in the suffrage and prohibition movement in the North, claimed that the tavern is "the Negro's center of power. Better whisky and more of it is the rallying cry of great dark faced mobs." These sentiments were echoed by a writer for the *Atlanta Constitution*, who warned his readers against returning to a "terrible condition of affairs that prevailed when swarms of negroes, many of them drunk with whisky…roamed the country at large."[55]

Although consumed by millions of Americans, and despite its many millennia of use and deep cultural roots, it was outlawed in the United States with the passage of the 18th Amendment in 1919 and the supporting prohibition laws.

The effect was significantly different than the stated intent. As soon as prohibition laws were passed, the thriving alcohol economy was driven into the underground, helping to develop and empower criminal syndicates. It also made criminals out of otherwise law-abiding citizens who wanted to have a drink, caused the U.S. to lose millions in tax receipts and increased the consumption of hard liquor.

In 1932 John D. Rockefeller, initially an ardent proponent of alcohol prohibition and the 18th Amendment, wrote to Nicholas Butler, President of Columbia University, to explain how his views had changed over the course of the previous decade. The letter was reprinted that year on the front page of *The New York Times*. His ability to capture the mood and resignation of the country at the end of its experiment with the 18th amendment could describe much of the public's view towards marijuana prohibition today:

> When Prohibition was introduced, I hoped that it would be widely supported by public opinion and the day would soon come when the evil effects of alcohol would be recognized. I have slowly and reluctantly come to believe that this has not

been the result. Instead, drinking has generally increased; the speakeasy has replaced the saloon; a vast army of lawbreakers has appeared; many of our best citizens have openly ignored Prohibition; respect for the law has been greatly lessened; and crime has increased to a level never seen before.

It was in the wake of this major sea change that the United States passed the 21st Amendment to the Constitution, repealing Prohibition. It was December 5, 1933.

How that decision was implemented, and the effects from it, might prove instructive for those considering an end to marijuana prohibition today. A good place to start is the end. If prohibition was meant to curb the public's appetite for and access to alcohol, if it was going to reduce crime and improve the lives of Americans, how did life compare during and after prohibition?

One interesting finding is that the public's desire for the "strong stuff" declined after the end of prohibition. When beer and wine became legal again, the economies and efficiencies of the higher alcohol volume in hard liquor became less desirable. Most estimates place the potency of prohibition-era products at 150+ percent of the potency of products produced either before or after Prohibition.[56]

Another positive post-prohibition development, which might have seemed counterintuitive before the passage of the 18th Amendment, was the significant decline in murder rates following its repeal.

Violent crime skyrocketed during Prohibition. With the outrageous profits provided by the black market, with a number of unregulated outlaw criminal syndicates battling to control their share of it, and without access to the courts to resolve business disputes, homicide became a fundamental aspect of commercial success for Prohibition's criminal entrepreneurs.

From 1920 to 1933, America endured a horrific crime wave that ended only after Prohibition was repealed. As shown in the graph on page 80, the homicide rate dropped precipitously after the repeal of prohibition. The only other similar sustained spike in violent crime in the 20th century came immediately after Nixon's declared "War on Drugs" from 1970 to 1990.[57]

The repeal of Prohibition also created a significant increase in government revenue from taxes on alcohol. This was extremely important for a country still struggling in the depths of the Great Depression.

Tax receipts from liquor increased from 2 percent of federal revenues in 1933 to 13 percent in 1936. This did a lot to make up for significant losses in income tax revenue during the Depression; it also allowed the federal government to cut income tax rates for all but the very rich. In 1934, the government reduced effective income tax rates for all taxpayers with net incomes of $20,000 ($326,000 in 2011 dollars) or less.[58]

Although they do not comprise as great a percentage of federal revenues today, alcohol excise tax receipts are still impressive; in 2008 the federal government collected $9.5 billion and the states an additional $5.8 billion.[59]

It's clear then, that the end of alcohol prohibition didn't produce the feared results of increased crime and drunkenness, and in fact, had some very positive results in terms of decreased violent crime, decreased hard alcohol consumption, decreased federal spending and increased tax receipts—not to mention resolving the national cognitive dissonance arising from laws that were routinely and openly flouted.

The takeaway is that alcohol, with all of its many attendant problems, has been regulated, controlled and taxed so that an accepted balance has been struck between the inherent risks and dangers associated with it and the benefits derived from it.

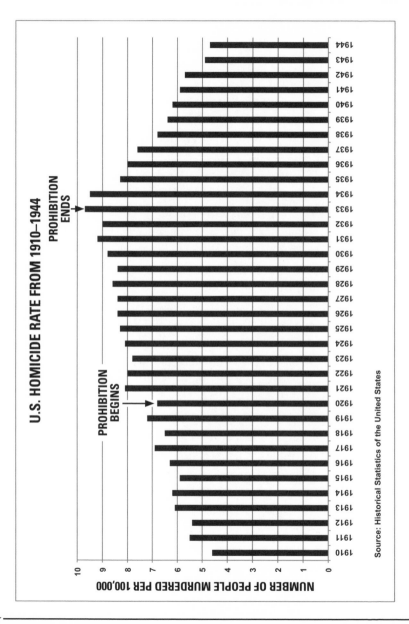

U.S. HOMICIDE RATE FROM 1910–1944

PROHIBITION ENDS

PROHIBITION BEGINS

NUMBER OF PEOPLE MURDERED PER 100,000

Source: Historical Statistics of the United States

Alcohol also happens to offer the readiest comparison to the topic of our book and is an excellent point of departure to look at these same issues as they relate to marijuana, the most widely used illicit substance in the world.

MARIJUANA

Worldwide, between 150 million and 200 million people have used marijuana within the last year, and there are 1.5 million acres under cultivation.[60] It is usually transported and sold as a dried green and brown mix of flowers, stems, seeds and leaves derived from the hemp plant *Cannabis sativa.* When consumed it is usually smoked in a cigarette or pipe, but can also be prepared in food or brewed as a tea. In a more concentrated, resinous form it is called hashish; and as a sticky black liquid, hash oil.[61]

It was first cultivated in central Asia more than 6,000 years ago and used for a variety of purposes, including oil, animal feed and fibers for fabrics as well as for its psychoactive properties. The first written reference comes from India nearly 4,000 years ago in the *Atharva Veda.* Its desired effects at that time varied widely, from increasing sexual desire and battlefield bravery, to dispelling boredom and making the harvest season more passable.[62] It has been used recreationally, medicinally and in religious ceremonies by people all over the globe for centuries.

The smoking of cannabis was introduced to the United States by Mexican laborers and by Caribbean and South American sailors in the beginning of the 20th century.[63] Its geographic reach was initially limited to the U.S./Mexico border and major ports like New Orleans and New York, and it then slowly made its way up through the West and major commercial centers along the Mississippi and even farther beyond to St. Louis, Kansas City, Cleveland, Detroit and Chicago.[64]

But it did not really bloom as a widespread recreational drug in the United States until long after it was prohibited in the 1930s.

Like alcohol, marijuana is a toxin whose molecules are able to pass the blood-brain barrier to produce feelings of pleasure and relaxation.

Tetrahydrocannabinol, or THC, is the main psychoactive substance found in the cannabis plant. It is the THC in marijuana that relieves pain, provides relaxation and euphoria and can even alter one's space-time perception. This organic compound can also produce anxiety, disorientation, fatigue and increased appetite.

It also has tantalizing possibilities for medicinal purposes, although these have not been fully explored due to its illegality. Recent studies, for example, indicate that THC could be used as a potential treatment for Alzheimer's disease and neuromuscular disorders like myasthenia gravis.

A clear danger associated with marijuana use is the increased risk of accident, and the deadliest marijuana accidents involve driving while under the influence of this drug. A French survey found that drivers who tested positive for marijuana were three times more likely to cause a fatal accident than sober drivers, and that there was a proportionately higher risk with increasing blood concentration of marijuana.[65] This same study found that marijuana was responsible for 2.5 percent of fatal accidents, compared to 28.6 percent for alcohol.

There is also a risk for addiction to marijuana, with 9 percent of users becoming dependent at some time. This compares to 15 percent for alcohol, 17 percent for cocaine, 23 percent for heroin, and 32 percent for tobacco.[66]

Negative health effects include bronchitis and other pulmonary disorders for long-term users.

However, unlike alcohol, the drive to prohibit marijuana was not motivated by efforts to reduce dependence, improve health outcomes and alleviate criminal activity in the general population. Its prohibition has a much more dubious provenance.

Like El Paso, which prohibited marijuana based on fears of Mexicans, 16 states west of the Mississippi, all with growing Mexican-American populations, banned the drug before 1930.[67] There was either direct or oblique references to the origin (Mexico), the users (Mexican) and the effects (murderous or criminal impulses) in many of the states that considered legislation banning the drug.

In Montana, it was more direct. The following is from *The Montana Standard* when that state was considering the prohibition of marijuana in 1929:

There was fun in the House Health Committee during the week when the Marihuana bill came up for consideration. Marihuana is Mexican opium, a plant used by Mexicans and cultivated for sale by Indians. "When some beet field peon takes a few rares of this stuff," explained Dr. Fred Fulsher of Mineral County, "he thinks he has just been elected president of Mexico so he starts out to execute all his political enemies. I understand that over in Butte where the Mexicans often go for the winter they stage imaginary bullfights in the 'Bower of Roses' or put on tournaments for the favor of 'Spanish Rose' after a couple of whiffs of Marijuana. The Silver Bow and Yellowstone delegations both deplore these international complications" Everybody laughed and the bill was recommended for passage.[68]

The first national law regulating marijuana use was the Marihuana Tax Act, passed in 1937. The fear of murderous Mexicans crazed on dope was again central to persuading America that the drug needed to be outlawed. During Congressional hearings, Harry Anslinger, the U.S. Commissioner of Narcotics, read a letter from the editor of *The Daily Courier* in Alamosa, Colorado, that contained this passage:

Two weeks ago a sex-mad degenerate, named Lee Fernandez, brutally attacked a young Alamosa girl. He was convicted of assault with intent to rape and sentenced to 10 to 14 years in the state penitentiary. Police officers here know definitely that Fernandez was under the influence of marihuana…

I wish I could show you what a small [amount of] marihuana can do to one of our degenerate Spanish-speaking residents. That's why our problem is so great; the greatest percentage of our population is composed of Spanish-speaking persons, most of who are low mentally, because of social and racial conditions.[69]

The act passed Congress with minimal debate and consideration. The comments of the American Medical Association (AMA), which opposed the bill, were disregarded and misrepresented (Congress was told that the AMA was in support) and when a congressman asked the speaker what was contained in the bill, he replied, "It has something to do with something that is called marihuana. I believe it is a narcotic of some kind."[70]

Possession of the drug now became a federal crime.[71]

The next 75 years would show that—like the 18th Amendment before it—the prohibition of marijuana failed to meet its most basic goals.

From 1975 to 2010, American high school children's marijuana habits have been monitored by the University of Michigan's "Monitoring the Future" study. In those 35 years, the study shows that the billions of dollars spent on marijuana prohibition have been an abject failure—that is, if keeping kids away from drugs is one of the objectives.

From 1975 to 2010, a consistent 80 to 85 percent of high school 12th graders have reported that marijuana is "fairly easy" or "very easy" to get. As could be expected, the consistent findings in access are coupled with sustained rates of use. In 1975, 40 percent of 12th graders reported using marijuana. In the intervening 35 years the numbers go up or down a few points in a given year, but the story remains largely the same. In 2010, the number of seniors getting high was 35 percent.[72] This, while the use among teenagers of alcohol—a legal, regulated drug—continues to plummet. The year 2010 marks the lowest level of alcohol use since the study's inception in 1975.[73]

Whether we look at use, experimentation with "harder stuff," violence or budgets, it is clear that problems related to marijuana prohibition have overshadowed any real threat posed by the drug itself. Tens of thousands murdered in drug crimes, the hundreds of thousands imprisoned, the millions arrested and the billions ineffectually spent produce a distorted, magnified image of our experience with alcohol prohibition.

While difficult to extricate marijuana numbers from total drug budgets, the amount spent on the war on drugs is telling, especially when considering that marijuana makes up the lion's share of what is produced, transited, distributed, sold and consumed in the U.S. drug market.

In a ground-breaking 2010 *Associated Press* report, Martha Mendoza found that the U.S. has spent over $1 trillion on the drug war since it was first declared in the Nixon administration. Today America's drug-fighting budget is over $15 billion a year, 31 times Nixon's budget, even when adjusted for inflation.[74]

The U.S. Drug Czar, Gil Kerlikowski, admitted that the war had been a failure. "In the grand scheme, it has not been successful," Kerlikowske told the *Associated Press*. "Forty years later, the concern about drugs and drug problems is, if anything, magnified, intensified."[75]

In her report, Martha Mendoza outlined where the money on the drug war has gone:

★ $20 billion to fight the drug gangs in their home countries. In Colombia, for example, the United States has spent more than $6 billion, while coca cultivation increased and trafficking moved to Mexico, along with the violence.

★ $33 billion in marketing "Just Say No"-style messages to America's youth and other prevention programs. High school students report the same rates of illegal drug use as they did in 1970, and the Centers for Disease Control and Prevention say drug overdoses have "risen steadily" since the early 1970s to more than 20,000 in 2010.

★ $49 billion for law enforcement along America's borders to cut off the flow of illegal drugs. This year, 25 million Americans will snort, swallow, inject and smoke illicit drugs, about 10 million more than in 1970, with the bulk of those drugs being imported from Mexico.

★ $121 billion to arrest more than 37 million nonviolent drug offenders, about 10 million of them for possession of marijuana. Studies show that jail time tends to increase drug abuse.

★ $450 billion to lock those people up in federal prisons. Last year, half of all federal prisoners in the U.S. were serving sentences for drug offenses.[76]

These are just the costs in dollars and time. They don't begin to show the impact these laws and policies have had on people or the devastation wrought on entire cities and countries.

And one drug has been central to this. "We're not winning the battle," Arizona Attorney General Terry Goddard told lawmakers at a 2009 congressional hearing. "The violence that we see in Mexico is fueled 65 to 70 percent by the trade in one drug: marijuana."[77]

CHAPTER 9

REGULATED, CONTROLLED AND TAXED– A BETTER MARIJUANA POLICY

If, like alcohol prohibition, marijuana prohibition has led to more harm than good—more lives destroyed, more money spent, more tax revenues foregone—then does it make sense to repeal its prohibition and treat marijuana more like alcohol?

Let's look at the benefits.

REDUCE CRIME IN MEXICO

One of the great ironies of marijuana prohibition is that at its root was a fear of the murderous and criminal tendencies that its use might incite, especially in Mexicans and those of Mexican descent. It is now obvious that it was the prohibition of marijuana, not its use, that has led to crime, violence and the rise of super-criminal syndicates throughout the world.

And no country has been more greatly devastated by the murder and criminality unleashed by prohibition than Mexico.

In the most recent campaign on the war on drugs in Mexico, starting with the Calderón presidency in 2006, more than 40,000 Mexicans have been killed. In Juárez alone, the number is close to 10,000.

While marijuana is not the only drug being transited through Mexico and across the border at Juárez for sale and consumption in the United States, it is the most central to the Mexican drug trade.

First, marijuana comprises a significant percentage of cartel revenues, anywhere from 30 to 60 percent, depending on which of the many official U.S. and Mexican estimates published over the last five years is used.

Second, as *The Wall Street Journal's* David Luhnow explains, marijuana is a safe, consistent producer on the cartels' balance sheets:

> If a cocaine shipment is seized, the Mexican gang has to write off the expected profits from the shipment and the cost of paying Colombian suppliers, meaning they lose twice. But because gangs here grow their own marijuana, it's easier to absorb the losses from a seizure. Cartels also own the land where the marijuana is grown, meaning they can cheaply grow more supply rather than have to fork over more money to the Colombians for the next shipment of cocaine.[78]

Less revenue, by an estimated $8 billion to $10 billion annually, means fewer resources to arm cartels, to hire new recruits, to buy politicians and judges, and to act with impunity throughout many regions of the country. Also, taking away this cornerstone of cartel finances destabilizes their operations and gives law enforcement a greater chance at success.

When alcohol prohibition was repealed, the mob didn't go away. But its influence in America, its ability to terrorize and control cities like Chicago, diminished considerably.

But the effects of prohibition, whether it is on booze or dope, are the same. This description of 1920s Chicago could describe Juárez today:

> The smuggling laws gave these criminals huge amounts of power, which they used to intimidate and effectively absorb the city government. Facing a choice between being killed or being enriched, city officials chose the latter. City government shifted from controlling the criminals to being an arm of criminal power. In the meantime, various criminal gangs competed with each other for power.[79]

So while the cartels won't magically disappear if their share of the marijuana trade evaporates, just as the mobsters in Chicago didn't disappear after their command of the liquor trade ended, they will become a much more manageable problem for Mexico. This will give the country a fighting chance to develop the social, economic and judicial infrastructure that will allow it to establish rule of law and civic institutions that demand respect, instead of contempt, from its citizens.

REDUCE CRIME IN THE U.S.

In 2009, the United States arrested 758,593 of its own adult citizens for merely possessing marijuana. That a negotiation of goods for money between two consenting adults—when the goods in question are the product of an abundant weed whose effects, while not inconsiderable, still pale in comparison to legal toxins—can result in the arrest of both parties, is stunning.

These arrestees are now permanently scarred and marked in the systems of justice, employment and social standing. Their chance of becoming productive members of society is now diminished. And as recourse for employment and upward mobility fade, the alternatives of crime and illicit activity become more obvious.

Then there are those who bear the full brute force of the law when they haven't done a thing to deserve it. The case of Cheye Calvo illustrates this and the rising trend of paramilitary police raids in the U.S. In an effort to make a bust, police completed the delivery of an intercepted package of drugs to Calvo's home in Prince George's County, Maryland. When his mother-in-law came out to bring the package inside, the police SWAT team assaulted the home, forcing their way inside and killing both of Calvo's dogs. Only after Calvo and his mother-in-law had been handcuffed for hours did the police realize that they had made a mistake; Calvo was never the intended recipient of the package.[80]

As Radley Balko writes in a white paper on the subject:

> These increasingly frequent raids, 40,000 per year by one estimate, are needlessly subjecting nonviolent drug offenders, bystanders, and wrongly targeted civilians to the terror of having their homes invaded while they're sleeping, usually by teams of heavily armed paramilitary units dressed not as police officers but as soldiers. These raids bring unnecessary violence and provocation to nonviolent drug offenders, many of whom were guilty of only misdemeanors. The raids terrorize innocents when police mistakenly target the wrong residence. And they have resulted in dozens of needless deaths and injuries, not only of drug offenders, but also of police officers, children, bystanders, and innocent suspects.[81]

The current regime also prevents those who need treatment, the estimated 9 percent of users who form a dependence on marijuana, from seeking care. If possession of the drug is a federal crime, how are they supposed to seek help without getting arrested?

It is no accident that the United States, with the largest marijuana market and the most draconian marijuana laws in the world, imprisons more people than any other country. By 2008, we were imprisoning more than 1 out of every 100 citizens, putting 1.6 million of our fellow citizens behind bars.

Another troubling aspect of the domestic prosecution of marijuana prohibition laws is the disparity in the people who are affected. One in 36 Hispanic adults is behind bars, and one in 15 Black adults is, too. It gets worse with younger men: one in nine Black men between the ages of 20 and 34 is behind bars. The average for all ethnicities in the U.S. is 1 for every 100. Not all of these people are in jail because of marijuana possession, but arrest statistics in New York show that marijuana prohibition disproportionately affects minority communities.

In 2010, over 50,000 New Yorkers were arrested for marijuana possession. Of those arrested, 86 percent were Black and Latino, even though national surveys show that Whites use in greater numbers.

The crackdown on marijuana crimes in New York has taken place during the term of Michael Bloomberg, who when asked if he had used marijuana responded, "You bet I did, and I enjoyed it." The injustice of a white man—one who has admitted using, and enjoying, marijuana— overseeing the most zealous campaign of marijuana prosecution in the world (no other city prosecutes more of its citizens for this offense), one that ends up disproportionately impacting Blacks and Latinos, is glaring. And to add insult to injury, New Yorkers must pay, through taxes, the price to make all of these arrests. The cost of prosecuting this offense in New York City alone is estimated to range from $53 million to $88 million annually.

This disparity in arrests, and convictions, is borne out nationally. In Chicago, nearly nine of every ten people who end up guilty of possessing marijuana are Black men.

Regulating and controlling the production and sale of marijuana will not only decrease costly arrests and imprisonment, but it will have the further benefit of reducing the disparity in arrests among races and ethnicities. It will also increase respect for the law as it resolves the disconnect between what the law says about marijuana and what is actually observed by the average citizen. As Albert Einstein said about alcohol prohibition, "Nothing is more destructive of respect for the government and the law of the land than passing laws which cannot be enforced."[82] Certainly the over 100 million Americans who have used marijuana in their lifetimes can testify to that.

CUT COSTS, RAISE REVENUES

As seen in the example of New York City, the cost to prosecute marijuana prohibition is not cheap. Nationally, it is assumed that the cost is close to $9 billion annually. On the other side of the ledger, states could expect to collect almost $3 billion in new taxes and the federal government nearly $6 billion if marijuana was taxed at rates comparable to alcohol and tobacco.[83]

As governments at all levels desperately search for services to cut and revenues to raise, a rational policy of regulation and taxation of marijuana sales could provide much needed help. Think of the number of local police officers, federal agents, judges, court personnel, prison guards and parole officers involved in attempting to uphold this prohibition against marijuana. Regulating and controlling the market would reduce the police power of the government for what is widely recognized as a trifling crime, allow it to focus resources on greater need, and generate additional tax revenue.

So with savings and additional revenues totaling nearly $18 billion, what could we use that money for? Some significant part of this money could cover public health costs related to the negative effects of marijuana. An even greater amount could be spent educating the public, especially children and teenagers, on the harms associated with marijuana.

A good example of regulating a toxin to reduce harmful effects is cigarettes. Along with higher cigarette taxes, public health advertisements have had a considerable impact on tobacco consumption in the U.S. Today 19 percent of Americans smoke, less than half the number in 1965.[84]

REDUCE MARIJUANA USE BY CHILDREN

In an unregulated black market, the dealers decide who their clients will be. In the case of marijuana, that means that children become a valuable customer base.

According to a 2003 Department of Justice study, over 40 percent of children in grades nine through 12 had used marijuana. An alarming 10 percent had tried marijuana for the first time *before* the age of 13. This is even more alarming when you consider that these young, still-developing brains are exposed to a drug which can interfere with short-term memory, learning, and psychomotor skills.[85]

In addition, the Department of Justice (DOJ) estimates that there are over 900,000 teen drug dealers in our country. You can imagine that the easiest type of customer for these teens to sell to is another teen, or even a preteen. Drug dealers don't check for ID. In 2010, 81 percent of 12th graders said marijuana was "fairly easy or very easy" to acquire. It's also no coincidence that the DOJ estimates that there are roughly the same number of teenagers carrying guns as there are dealing drugs. In 2004, homicide was the second-leading cause of death for young people ages 10 to 24, with 81 percent shot dead.[86] How many teens are selling Budweiser and Marlboro and packing heat to protect their share of their high school alcohol or cigarette market?

If marijuana were sold in a regulated and controlled manner, the government, not the dealers, would decide who could buy and who would not be able to buy. It is worth noting that in the Netherlands, where marijuana use is regulated so that only adults over the age of 18 can purchase and consume the drug, the rate of use for children under the age of 15 is 7 percent. In the U.S., with some of the world's harshest marijuana laws, the rate of use for this same group is 20 percent.[87]

While some teenagers would find a way to acquire marijuana in a regulated market, much as they do with alcohol and tobacco today, these scofflaws would be the marginal exception. In 2009, more 10th graders used marijuana than used tobacco.[88] Regulating and controlling the market would go a long way towards stemming the out-of-control use and accompanying violence that are part and parcel of an unregulated black market in our nation's schools.

CLOSE THE GATEWAY

A popular theory is that marijuana is a "gateway drug," meaning that the use of this drug will lead to the use of other, harder drugs.

This is true, but has little or nothing to do with the intrinsic properties of marijuana and much more to do with the current marketplace for illegal drugs.

In 1999, the White House Office of National Drug Control Policy asked the Institute of Medicine (IOM) to assess this theory. The IOM report concluded that "the legal status of marijuana makes it a gateway drug." Or, as a 1972 report commissioned by President Nixon put it, because marijuana is an illegal drug, "[the user] may eventually view himself as a drug user and be willing to experiment with other drugs which are approved by his peer group."[89]

Another way to look at it is through the prism of the black market. To buy marijuana in the U.S., you must purchase it from an illegal drug dealer. There is a good chance that that same dealer is also selling other, harder drugs like cocaine, heroin and methamphetamines. It is in his interests to get you to buy these other offerings.

If you buy dope in a coffee shop in Amsterdam, where marijuana is decriminalized, you can only add a coffee or a hot chocolate to your order. In the U.S., your choices often include an array of toxic recreational drugs. It is no wonder then that in the Netherlands the lifetime prevalence of cocaine use is 2 percent while in the U.S. it is 16 percent.[90] The Dutch have effectively closed the gateway from marijuana to other drugs.

Regulate marijuana and you remove other more pernicious options from the 42 percent of Americans who try marijuana in their lifetime.

Another related harm associated with the prohibition of marijuana is that its prohibition increases the likelihood that producers will develop higher levels of potency and traffickers will truck in loads with greater payoffs. To again use alcohol prohibition as the analogy that illustrates the fundamental problem with marijuana prohibition:

> A number of observers of Prohibition noted that the potency of alcoholic products rose. Not only did producers and consumers switch to stronger alcoholic beverages (from beer to whiskey), but producers supplied stronger forms of particular beverages, such as fortified wine. The typical beer, wine, or whiskey contained a higher percentage of alcohol by volume during Prohibition than it did before or after. Fisher, for example, referred to "White Mule Whiskey," a name that clearly indicates that the product had quite a kick. Most estimates place the potency of prohibition-era products at 150+ percent of the potency of products produced either before or after Prohibition.[91]

From 1980 to 1997, the potency of marijuana (concentration of delta9-THC) has gone from 1.5 percent to 4.5 percent, an almost 200 percent increase in potency over just 17 years.[92] By 2008, the potency had risen to 8.8 percent, an increase of nearly 500 percent![93]

In a regulated, controlled market, the government, not the growers and marketers, would decide the limits of potency.

THE LEAST BAD SOLUTION

Lest the reader think that we endorse marijuana use by advocating a regulated and controlled marijuana market as an alternative to the status quo, let's be clear by describing this as the best of a number of terrible alternatives.

The ideal option under the current regime of prohibition would be to somehow magically stop consumption, ending all of the problems associated with demand and supply in a black market. But this has proven to be unattainable over the last 100 years. U.S. demand for marijuana is insatiable and shows no signs of declining, despite billions of dollars spent to reduce it. Likewise, production, domestically and internationally, has always managed to keep pace, hewing closely to the most fundamental law of economics: where there is a demand, there will be a supply.

It is in recognition of this that a number of global leaders in the fields of politics, business and non-governmental organizations signed on to the Global Commission on Drug Policy's June 2011 report. This document advocates, among other things, ending prohibition on marijuana. In an opinion piece in *The Wall Street Journal*, George Shultz, former Secretary of State under President Ronald Reagan, and Paul Volker, former Federal Reserve Chairman under Presidents Reagan and Carter, explained their support for the report as a means to "find our way to a less costly and more effective method of discouraging drug use, cutting down the power of organized crime, providing better treatment and minimizing negative societal effects."[94]

GOING FORWARD

It is clearly not enough to decriminalize marijuana, that is, to make consumption legal while leaving production and distribution illegal. That might resolve some of the issues relating to arrest rates for possession, but it would leave enormous power in the hands of the cartels and criminals.

Instead, we must accept the difficult choice of regulating, controlling and taxing the entire cycle of the marijuana market, from production to transit, from distribution to sale.

The clearest, cleanest analogy from which to build a model for a regulated marijuana market is the regulated alcohol market. The rough outlines of its implementation for marijuana would involve:

★ Restricting sale of marijuana to adults; and requiring proof of age and identification before a customer is allowed to purchase.

★ Licensing producers, distributors and sellers to ensure that potency and quality are regulated, as well as to ensure that there is payment of taxes and fees. In addition, producers, distributors and sellers would have to keep their facilities apart from schools, daycares, churches and other incompatible land uses.

★ Conducting an aggressive advertising campaign that outlines the dangers associated with marijuana use, with a strong focus on deterring driving under the influence and use by children.

★ Limiting smoking of marijuana to private residences and non-public spaces.

★ Restricting advertisement of marijuana along the lines of tobacco products, where it is prohibited from appealing to children and the dangers of use are clearly stated.

There are sure to be problems with any implementation of regulation. There is no foolproof safeguard to prevent every single child from gaining access; there will be those whose use will lead to dependence; some lower level of black market will persist; and criminals who now profit in the black market may evolve into winners in a new, regulated market.

But at some point, sooner rather than later, we must admit that our current course has, in the words of our drug czar, "not been successful," it has made things worse for those who are most vulnerable (children and addicts), has led to bloated enforcement budgets at every level of government, has invited contempt for law and justice, has destroyed thousands of lives, and has left us billions of dollars poorer as a result.

At some point parenting and personal responsibility must become the domain of the individual and not the state. At some point we must challenge our elected leaders to enact laws that reflect reality and not an unattainable ideology. At some point we must own up to our complicity in the murder and brutality in Juárez and limit the inputs that we control. And at some point we must come to a reckoning, much the same way we did 80 years ago, and repeal a prohibition that does more harm than good.

AFTERWORD

The man who launched the war against the drug cartels in Mexico, who justified the violence and the carnage as a necessary condition of regaining control of his country, who—even after the Villas de Salvarcar massacre in 2010 where 13 children were murdered at a birthday party—said that the massacres only "reinforce our determination to fight and defeat those criminals...It is painful, but there is no alternative," has come to the conclusion that the drug war cannot be won.

In a seismic shift in rhetoric and course, President Felipe Calderón said this September that a prohibition-centered policy could not achieve its goals. "Decision-makers," he said, surely referring to himself and his counterpart in the White House, "must look for other solutions, including market alternatives, to reduce the astronomical profits of these criminal organizations."

Edna Jaime, a Mexican political analyst says Calderón is "clearly referring to legalization when speaking of 'market alternatives,' perhaps considering it 'too compromising to spell it out with all its letters.'"[95]

After years of reflexively rejecting previous calls for rethinking drug policy, Calderón has come to the conclusion that the consequences and ineffectiveness of the current policy have become too costly to ignore.

His is only the latest, although given what's happened in Mexico and Juárez in his nearly six years in office, perhaps the most important voice in a growing chorus of global leaders who recognize that the drug war, especially the prohibition of marijuana, is a costly failure.

It has been almost three years since the El Paso City Council sounded a national alarm about the brutal violence in Juárez and asked for an "open and honest debate" about U.S. drug policy and its impact on Juárez.

Every day the headlines mark the daily death count in Juárez's drug war, a war in which no one wins and everyone loses. Since 2008—as I finalize this Afterword in September 2011—more than 9,000 people have been murdered in Juárez. Cartel members and innocents alike are killed; the governments of the U.S. and Mexico spend billions of our tax dollars on marijuana prohibition; and yet my daughter, a sophomore in high school, reports that it is widely available at school and has been since the 7th grade—a finding that is confirmed by national studies showing that marijuana is more available for many children than cigarettes or beer. If our current drug policy has not successfully shielded my children from the ability to access drugs, how can I—how can we—support a policy that accepts the terror in Juárez, the drug-trade killings in U.S. inner-cities and the absolute waste of billions of taxpayer dollars as collateral damage in a war that is supposedly being waged to keep drugs out of the hands of our kids?

And yet, unfortunately, the conclusion reached by Calderón, his two predecessors as President of Mexico, former secretary of state George Shultz and leaders from around the globe is still not politically acceptable for those with the power to change things for the better—the "decision-makers" that Calderón refers to. Faced with the drug war death toll in Mexico, faced with the high costs of the drug war and faced with the failures of the existing drug war policies, politicians and policymakers in both Mexico and the United States have responded by doing more of the same: committing additional billions of dollars to a 40-year strategy that has failed the citizens of both countries.

If Washington won't do anything different, if Mexico City won't do anything different, then it is up to us—the citizens of the border who understand the futility and tragedy of this current policy first hand—to lead the way.

★ Susie Byrd

ENDNOTES

INTRODUCTION

¹ Molloy, Molly. "Juárez Murders: Impunity Regardless of Gender," *Grassroots Press*, May 12, 2010. grass-roots-press.com/2010/05/12/3615/.

² Crowder, David. "Warnings Work, Votes Change, Veto Override Fails." *NewspaperTree: El Paso's Online Newspaper*, January 13, 2009. newspapertree.com/news/3322-with-a-tie-city-council-fails-to-override-mayoral-veto-of-juarez-drug-war-resolution.

CHAPTER 1

³ See graph on page 104, entitled Murders in Juárez, 1993–2010.

⁴ "President Felipe Calderón in Juárez," *Borderland Beat: Reporting on the Mexican Cartel Drug War,* February 12, 2010. borderlandbeat. com/2010/02/police-disperse-protest-against.html

⁵ "Opportunity Lost," *The Economist*, February 14, 2002. economist. com/node/989077

⁶ Halkin, Alex. "Living Juárez" (work in progress), film, Chiapas Media Project, interchangeproductions.org/documentary-film/living-juarez/

⁷ Grillo, Ioan. "Mexico Cracking Down on Drug Violence," *Associated Press*, December 12, 2006.

⁸ Corchado, Alfredo. "Calderón Sends Mexican Troops, Federal Police into Ciudad Juárez," *Dallas Morning News*, March 27, 2008.

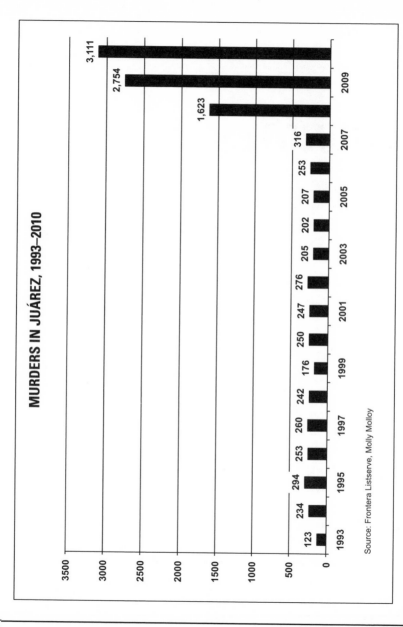

MURDERS IN JUÁREZ, 1993–2010

Year	Murders
1993	123
1994	234
1995	294
1996	253
1997	260
1998	242
1999	176
2000	250
2001	247
2002	276
2003	205
2004	202
2005	207
2006	253
2007	316
2008	1,623
2009	2,754
2010	3,111

Source: Frontera Listserve, Molly Molloy

[9] Schmall, Emily. "Mexico Mulls Dissolving Overwhelmed City Police Forces," *AOLNEWS.COM*, August 25, 2010. aolnews.com/2010/08/25/mexico-mulls-dissolving-overwhelmed-city-police-forces/

CHAPTER 2

[10] U.S. Department of Justice, National Drug Intelligence Center, *Chicago High Intensity Drug Trafficking Area: Drug Market Analysis 2010* (Washington, DC: May 2010), 1. justice.gov/ndic/pubs40/40385/index.htm

[11] Fainaru, Steve and William Booth. "Flores Drug Indictment Gives Clues to Mexican Cartels' Networks in the U.S." *The Washington Post,* December 31, 2009. washingtonpost.com/wp-dyn/content/article/2009/12/30/AR2009123001206.html

[12] See chart on page 106, entitled Costs and Revenues Associated with Trafficking Marijuana from Mexico to the U.S. Through Juárez Plaza.

[13] The drug trade insider indicated that in Mexico revenues and expenses are valued in kilograms but then converted to pounds once they reach the U.S. In order to make the analysis more understandable, we converted all values to pounds.

[14] Court Transcripts for United States of America vs. Manuel Chavez-Betancourt, Fernando Ontiveros-Arambula, March 4, 2010, Volume 8 of 13, Document 846, Jury Trial Before the Honorable David Briones, United States District Judge, and a Jury, 136.

[15] Court Transcripts for *United States of America vs. Manuel Chavez-Betancourt, Fernando Ontiveros-Arambula,* Jury Trial Before the Honorable David Briones, United States District Judge, and a Jury, (El Paso, Texas, Volume 8 of 13, Document 846, March 4, 2010), 136.

[16] Court Transcripts for *United States of America vs. Manuel Chavez-Betancourt, Fernando Ontiveros-Arambula,* Jury Trial Before the

Costs and Revenues Associated with Trafficking Marijuana from Mexico to the U.S. Through Juárez Plaza						
	Drug Trade Insider		Agency (Document		Miscelleanous	
	Low	High	Low	High	Low	High
Payment to grower	$23/lb	$36/lb	No public data			$25/pound (1)
Freight from grow site to Juárez	$14/lb	$23/lb	No public data			
Wholesale value in Juárez	$73/lb	$91/lb	$75/lb	$125/lb		
Freight from Juárez to El Paso	$40/lb	$60/lb	No public data			
Payment to Customs agent to protect load	$10/lb or less for loads over 1,000 lbs		No public data			
Wholesale value in El Paso	$240/lb	$260/lb	$280/lb	$350/lb	$200/lb	$300/lb (2)
Freight to Chicago	$75/lb	$100/lb	No public data		price varies according to distance (3)	
Wholesale Value in Chicago	$550/lb	$700/lb	$800/lb	$1,000/lb	$500/lb	$1,050/lb (4)
Freight for Bulk Cash Back to Mexico (Charge based on percent of the amount of money being shipped)	2%	3%	No public data		2%	3% (5)

Note: The insider provided all the values in Mexico in kilograms, noting that when the product crosses over the values are converted to pounds. For ease in understanding the information, the above values were converted to pounds.

Note: The insider provided information about a normal load of marijuana of average grade. The DEA estimates include the full range of prices inclusive of all products types.

(1) Fainaru, Steve and William Booth, "Cartels Face an Economic Battle," *Washington Post*, October 7, 2009. http://www.washingtonpost.com/wp-dyn/content/article/2009/10/06/AR2009100603847.html

(2) Narcotic News. http://www.narcoticnews.com/Marijuana-Prices-in-the-U.S.A.php

(3) Testimony of Paul Quaintance, Court Transcripts for United States of America vs. Manuel Chavez-Betancourt, Fernando Ontiveros-Arambula, Jury Trial Before the Honorable David Briones, United States District Judge, and a Jury, (El Paso, Texas, Volume 7 of 13, Document 845, March 3, 2010), 7-58.

(4) U.S. Drug Enforcement Administration Press Release, "11 Alleged Members of Juarez Drug Cartel Arrested in Chicago Investigation," September 30, 2008.

(5) Booth, William and Nick Miroff, "Stepped-Up Efforts by U.S., Mexico Fail to Stem Flow of Money South," *Washington Post*, August 25, 2010.http://www.washingtonpost.com/wp-dyn/content/article/2010/08/25/AR2010082506161.html?hpid=topnews

Honorable David Briones, United States District Judge, and a Jury, (El Paso, Texas, Volume 8 of 13, Document 846, March 4, 2010), 185.

[17] Stewart, Scott, "The Buffer Between Mexican Cartels and the U.S. Government," *STRATFOR: Global Intelligence*, August 17, 2011. stratfor.com/weekly/20110817-buffer-between-mexican-cartels-and-us-government

[18] Fitz, Marshall, "Border: Safer than Ever, A View from the U.S.-Mexico Border: Assessing the Past, Present and Future," *Tucsonsentinel. com: Independent Nonprofit Online News*, August 7, 2011. tucsonsentinel. com/opinion/report/080711_border_safer/border-safer-than-ever/

[19] "Law enforcement reporting and case initiation data show that Mexican Drug Trafficking Organizations control most of the wholesale cocaine, heroin, and methamphetamine distribution in the United States as well as much of the marijuana distribution." U.S. Department of Justice, National Drug Intelligence Center, *National Drug Threat Assessment 2010* (Washington, DC: February 2010), 9. justice.gov/ndic/pubs38/38661/index.htm

[20] Kilmer, Beau, Jonathan P. Caulkins, Rosalie Liccardo Pacula, Robert J. MacCoun and Peter H. Reuter, *Altered State? Assessing How Marijuana Legalization in California Could Influence Consumption and Public Budgets* (Santa Monica, CA: Rand Corporation, 2010): 19.

CHAPTER 3

[21] See chart on page 108, entitled Estimates of the Value and Size of the U.S. Market for Illegal Drugs.

[22] See chart on page 109, entitled Estimates of the Value and Size of the U.S. Market for Marijuana.

[23] See chart on page 109, entitled Estimated Income of Mexican Drug Cartels by Drug Type.

[24] U.S. Department of State, Bureau for International Narcotics and Law Enforcement Affairs, "Drug and Chemical Control, Volume

ESTIMATES OF THE VALUE AND SIZE OF THE U.S. MARKET FOR ILLEGAL DRUGS

	Year	Cocaine		Marijuana		Methamphetamine		Heroine		Total Retail Expenditures for All Four Drug Types
		Amount (Metric Tons)	Retail Value (Billions)	Amount (Metric Tons)	Retail Value (Billions)	Amount (Metric Tons)	Retail Value (Billions)	Amount (Metric Tons)	Retail Value (Billions)	
Abt Associates	2000	259	$36.0	1,047	$11.0	19.7	$5.4	13.3	$10.0	$62.4
Kilmer and Pacula, 2009	2005	381	$52.9	2,947	$17.0	32	$3.5	14	$7.2	$80.6
Kilmer, Caulkins, et al, 2010	2009	207	$30.0	3,300	$19.0*	19	$5.0	44	$20.0	$74.0
Office of National Drug Control Policy		330				110		20		
World Drug Report, 2010	2008	165	$35.0					20	$7.9	

*Assessment of value not provided in report but arrived at by using retail value from Kilmer and Pacula, 2009

ESTIMATES OF THE VALUE AND SIZE OF THE U.S. MARKET FOR MARIJUANA

	Year	Amount (Metric Tons)	Retail Value (Billions)
Abt Associates	2000	1,047	$11
DEA, unpublished, 2000	2000	4,270	
Drug Availability Steering Committee, 2002	2001	10,000-24,000	
Kilmer and Pacula, 2009	2005	2,947	$17
Dr. John Gettman, 2006	2005	9,830	$113
Kilmer, Caulkins, et al, 2010	2009	3,300	$19*
United Nations World Drug Report, 2009	2009	1,472-4,907	
Jeffry Miron, interview with CNBC	2010		$14
"How Big is the Marijuana Market,"CNBC	2010		$35-$40

*Assessment of value not provided in report but arrived at by using retail value from Kilmer and Pacula, 2009

ESTIMATED INCOME OF MEXICAN DRUG CARTELS BY DRUG TYPE

	Exports (Tons)		Value Added (In Billions)		Estimated Income	
	Low	High	Low	High	Low	High
Cocaine	165	320	$10,000	$15,000	$1,650	$4,800
Marijuana	1,000	2,000	$750	$1,500	$750	$3,000
Heroine	6	10	$50,000	$70,000	$300	$700
Methamphetamine	16	32	$10,000	$15,000	$160	$480
			Total Income:		$2,860	$8,980

Source: SAHMSA, DEA, CENAPI (Slide titled "Defining Your Enemy") presented by Alejandro Hope Pinsón, Director of International Affairs, Center for Research and National Security, Government of Mexico, at the 2010 Border Security Conference)

1" in *International Narcotics Control Strategy Report*, (Washington, DC: March 2010), 432. state.gov/documents/organization/137411.pdf

[25] In their retraction, the Office of National Drug Control Policy in their published press statement said that previous estimates were "based on data from 1997, was derived from models of marijuana yield and the nature of the drug trafficking business that are dated and may no longer apply. There have been changes in the volume and type of drugs trafficked by these organizations, as well as changes in their markets. Further, Mexican cartels derive revenue from criminal activities such as kidnapping, extortion, and human trafficking. Because of the variety and scope of the cartels' business, and its illicit and purposefully obscured nature, determining the precise percentage of revenues from marijuana is problematic."

The White House Office of National Drug Control Policy, "ONDCP Statement on Mexican Drug Trafficking Organization Profits from Marijuana," September 16, 2010.

[26] Placido, Anthony P. (Assistant Administrator for Intelligence, Drug Enforcement Administration) and Kevin L. Perkins (Assistant Director, Criminal Investigative Division, Federal Bureau of Investigation), "Drug Trafficking Violence in Mexico: Implications for the United States," Statement for the Record Presented to the U.S. Senate Caucus on International Narcotics Control, May 5, 2010.

[27] See chart on page 111, entitled Product Losses.

[28] Miron, Jeffrey A., *The Budgetary Implications of Drug Prohibition* (February 2010), 1. economics.harvard.edu/faculty/miron/files/budgetpercent202010percent20Final.pdf

[29] Pinsón, Alejandro Hope (Director of International Affairs, Center for Research and National Security (CISEN), Government of Mexico), "Defining Your Enemy," Speech Presented at the annual Border Security Conference hosted by the University of Texas at El Paso, August 12, 2010.

PRODUCT LOSSES

MARIJUANA LOSSES		Converted to Metric Tons
Marijuana seized in USA in kilograms	1,471,921	1,472
Marijuana seized in Mexico in kilograms	1,657,853	1,658
Marijuana eradicated in Mexico in hectares*	18,663	18,663
Marijuana plants eradicated in USA**	8,013,308	1,588
	TOTAL	21,909

*Note: This is a conservative estimate of 1,000 kilograms per hectar (kg/ha) crop yield. The World Drug Report 2009 (page 93, footnote) states, "The typical yield for outdoor cannabis varies between 470 kg/ha without irrigation to 5,000 hg/ha in well-tended gardens, with figures around 2,000 kg/ha typical for the situation in the USA and levels around 1,000 kg/ha typical for developing countries."

**Note: 450,986 were indoor plants and 7,562,322 were outdoor plants. According to Gettman, 200 grams comes from one outdoor plant and 100 grams from one indoor plant. The U.S. Government uses a figure of one pound produced per plant. For this calculation, we used Gettman's more conservative estimate.

CHAPTER 4

[30] Testimony of Jose Luis Terrazas, Court Transcripts for *United States of America vs. Manuel Chavez–Betancourt, Fernando Ontiveros–Arambula,* Jury Trial Before the Honorable David Briones, United States District Judge, and a Jury, (El Paso, Texas, Volume 5 of 13, Document 843, March 1, 2010), 231-264.

Testimony of Jose Luis Terrazas, Court Transcripts for *United States of America vs. Manuel Chavez–Betancourt, Fernando Ontiveros–Arambula,* Jury Trial Before the Honorable David Briones, United States District Judge, and a Jury, (El Paso, Texas, Volume 6 of 13, Document 844, March 2, 2010), 7-44.

Testimony of Jesus Armando Aranda, Court Transcripts for *United States of America vs. Manuel Chavez–Betancourt, Fernando Ontiveros–Arambula,* Jury Trial Before the Honorable David Briones, United States District Judge, and a Jury, (El Paso, Texas, Volume 6 of 13, Document 844, March 2, 2010), 124-266.

Testimony of Paul Quaintance, Court Transcripts for *United States of America vs. Manuel Chavez–Betancourt, Fernando Ontiveros–Arambula,* Jury Trial Before the Honorable David Briones, United States District Judge, and a Jury, (El Paso, Texas, Volume 7 of 13, Document 845, March 3, 2010), 7-58.

CHAPTER 5

[31] Dr. Tony Payan, an Associate Professor of Political Science at the University of Texas at El Paso with expertise in the field of international relations, with emphasis on U.S. Foreign Policy; Mexican foreign policy; U.S.-Mexico relations; and international relations theory on the border, interviewed sources that he has in the Juárez black market to obtain this information, July 21, 2011.

[32] Dr. Tony Payan, July 21, 2011.

[33] Dr. Tony Payan, July 21, 2011.

[34] Testimony of Jose Luis Terrazas, Court Transcripts for *United States of America vs. Manuel Chavez-Betancourt, Fernando Ontiveros-Arambula*, Jury Trial Before the Honorable David Briones, United States District Judge, and a Jury, (El Paso, Texas, Volume 6 of 13, Document 844, March 2, 2010), 22-23.

[35] El Paso Police Department, email to author, March 30, 2011.

[36] United Nations Office on Drugs and Crime, *World Drug Report 2011*, (United Nations Publication, Sales No. E.11.XI.10), 190.

CHAPTER 6

[37] Testimony of Jesus Armando Aranda, Court Transcripts for *United States of America vs. Manuel Chavez-Betancourt, Fernando Ontiveros-Arambula*, Jury Trial Before the Honorable David Briones, United States District Judge, and a Jury, (El Paso, Texas, Volume 6 of 13, Document 844, March 2, 2010), 164-166.

CHAPTER 7

[38] "Excerpts From President's Message on Drug Abuse Control," *The New York Times*, June 18, 1971, p. 22.

[39] "Excerpts From President's Message on Drug Abuse Control," *The New York Times*, June 18, 1971, p. 22.

[40] Fries, Arthur, Robert W. Anthony, Andrew Cseko, Jr., Carl C. Gaither and Erick Schulman, *The Price and Purity of Illicit Drugs, 1981–2007* (Alexandria, Virginia: Institute for Defense Analyses, 2008), 9.

[41] Johnston, L. D., O'Malley, P. M., Bachman, J. G., & Schulenberg, J. E. (2010). *Monitoring the Future. National Results on Adolescent Drug Use: Overview of Key Findings, 2009* (Bethesda, MD: National Institute on Drug Abuse. NIH Publication No. 10-7583, May 2010) 18-19.

[42] Johnston, L. D., O'Malley, P. M., Bachman, J. G., & Schulenberg, J. E. (2010). *Monitoring the Future. National Results on Adolescent Drug Use: Overview of Key Findings, 2009* (Bethesda, MD: National Institute

on Drug Abuse. NIH Publication No. 10-7583, May 2010*)* 18-19.

[43] U.S. Department of Justice, National Drug Intelligence Center, *National Drug Threat Assessment 2009* (Washington, DC: December 2008) justice.gov/ndic/pubs31/31379/index.htm

[44] Reuter, Peter. "How Can Domestic U.S. Drug Policy Help Mexcio?" in *Shared Responsibility: U.S.-Mexico Policy Options for Confronting Organized Crime,* ed. Eric L. Olson, Andrew Selee, and David Shirk, (Washington, DC: Woodrow Wilson International Center for Scholars, Mexico Institute, October 2010), 122.

[45] Carl, Tracy, "Progress is Mexico is Drenched in Blood," *Associated Press,* November 3, 2009.

[46] Miglierini, Julian, "Bodies Found as Mexicans March Against Drug Violence," *BBC News: Latin American and Caribbean,* April 7, 2011. bbc.co.uk/news/world-latin-america-12992664

CHAPTER 8

[47] "Crazed by a Weed, Man Murders," *El Paso Herald,* January 2, 1913.

[48] "EP Pharmacist Looks Back on 54 Years of Service," *El Paso Times,* October 12, 1971.

[49] Courtwright, David T., *Forces of Habit: Drugs and the Marking of the Modern World* (Cambridge, Massachusetts and London, England: Harvard University Press, 2001).

[50] Courtwright, David T., *Forces of Habit: Drugs and the Marking of the Modern World* (Cambridge, Massachusetts and London, England: Harvard University Press, 2001).

[51] Gately, Iain, *Drink: A Cultural History of Alcohol,* (New York, New York: Penguin Group, 2008).

[52] Gately, Iain, *Drink: A Cultural History of Alcohol,* (New York, New York: Penguin Group, 2008).

[53] R. J. Bonnie and C. H. Whitebread, *The Marihuana Conviction*

(Charlottesville: University of Virginia Press, 1974), 7.

[54] Wine Institute, "Wine Consumption in the U.S." Revised April 9, 2011. wineinstitute.org/resources/statistics/article86

[55] Okrent, Daniel, *Last Call: The Rise and Fall of Prohibition* (New York, New York: Scribner, A Division of Simon and Schuster, 2010).

[56] Thorton, Mark, "Cato Institute Policy Analysis No. 157: Alcohol Prohibition Was a Failure," Cato Institute, July 17, 1991. scribd.com/fullscreen/31267826

[57] Miron, Jeffrey. "Alcohol Prohibition," EH.Net Encyclopedia, ed. Robert Whaples, September 24, 2001. eh.net/encyclopedia/article/miron.prohibition.alcohol

[58] Boudreaux, Donald J., "Alcohol, Prohibition, and the Revenuers: The Great Depression's Income-Tax Revenue Reduction Paved the Way for the Repeal of Prohibition," Volume 58, Issue 1 of Foundation for Economic Freedom, January 2008. thefreemanonline.org/columns/thoughts-on-freedom-alcohol-prohibition-and-the-revenuers/

[59] Tax Policy Center, "Alcohol Tax Revenue," Urban Institute and Brookings Institute, October 22, 2010. taxpolicycenter.org/taxfacts/displayafact.cfm?Docid=399

Tax Policy Center, "Annual Federal Excise Tax Revenue by Type of Tax 1996-2009," Urban Institute and Brookings Institute, March 2, 2011. taxpolicycenter.org/taxfacts/displayafact.cfm?Docid=74&Topic2id=80

[60] United Nations Office on Drugs and Crime, *World Drug Report 2010* (United Nations Publication), 194.

[61] National Institute on Drug Abuse, "NIDA InfoFacts: Marijuana," Revised November 20101. drugabuse.gov/infofacts/marijuana.html

[62] Courtwright, David T., *Forces of Habit: Drugs and the Marking of the Modern World* (Cambridge, Massachusetts and London, England: Harvard University Press, 2001).

[63] Courtwright, David T., *Forces of Habit: Drugs and the Marking of*

the Modern World (Cambridge, Massachusetts and London, England: Harvard University Press, 2001).

[64] R. J. Bonnie and C. H. Whitebread, *The Marihuana Conviction* (Charlottesville: University of Virginia Press, 1974).

[65] Amerigian, Zoë, "Legalizing Marijuana: An Exit Strategy from the War on Drugs," Council on Hemispheric Affairs, April 19, 2011. coha.org/legalizing-pot-an-exit-strategy-from-the-war-on-drugs/

[66] Amerigian, Zoë, "Legalizing Marijuana: An Exit Strategy from the War on Drugs," Council on Hemispheric Affairs, April 19, 2011. coha.org/legalizing-pot-an-exit-strategy-from-the-war-on-drugs/

[67] Bonnie, R.J and Whitebread, II, C.H. "The Forbidden Fruit and the Tree of Knowledge: An Inquiry into the Legal History of American Marijuana Prohibition," Virginia Law Review (Volume 56, Number 6), October 1970. druglibrary.org/schaffer/LIBRARY/studies/vlr/vlr2.htm

[68] *The Montana Standard*, January 27, 1929, at 3, col. 2. druglibrary. org/schaffer/LIBRARY/studies/vlr/vlr2.htm

[69] Anslinger, H.J. (Commissioner of Narcotics), "The Marihuana Tax Act of 1937," Transcripts of Congressional Hearings.

[70] Bonnie, Richard J and Charles H Whitebread II, *The Marijuana Conviction: A History of Marijuana Prohibition in the United States* (Lindesmith Center Drug Policy Classic, 1999), 174.

[71] Bonnie, Richard J and Charles H Whitebread II, *The Marijuana Conviction: A History of Marijuana Prohibition in the United States* (Lindesmith Center Drug Policy Classic, 1999), 175.

[72] Johnston, L. D., O'Malley, P. M., Bachman, J. G., & Schulenberg, J. E, *Monitoring the Future: National Results on Adolescent Drug Use: Overview of Key Findings, 2010.* (Ann Arbor: Institute for Social Research, The University of Michigan, 2011), 12-13.

[73] "Marijuana Use is Rising; Ecstasy Use is Beginning to Rise; and Alcohol Use is Declining among U.S. Teens," Press Release from The University of Michigan about *Monitoring the Future* survey, December

14, 2010. monitoringthefuture.org/pressreleases/10drugpr.pdf

[74] Mendoza, Martha, "US Drug War has Met None of Its Goals," *Associated Press,* May 13, 2010.

[75] Mendoza, Martha, "US Drug War has Met None of Its Goals," *Associated Press,* May 13, 2010.

[76] Mendoza, Martha, "US Drug War has Met None of Its Goals," *Associated Press,* May 13, 2010.

[77] "Senators Want to Fight Mexican Drug Cartels' Expanding Influence," *CNN.com,* March 17, 2009. articles.cnn.com/2009-03-17/politics/mexican.drug.war_1_cartels-mexican-border-ciudad-juarez?_s=PM:POLITICS

CHAPTER 9

[78] Luhnow, David, "Saving Mexico," *The Wall Street Journal,* December 26, 2009.

[79] Friedman, Greg, "Mexico: On the Road to a Failed State," *STRATFOR: Global Intelligence*, May 13, 2008. stratfor.com/weekly/mexico_road_failed_state

[80] Balko, Radley, "4.5 SWAT Raids per Day, Maryland's SWAT Transparency Bill Produces Its First Disturbing Results," *Reason Magazine,* March 1, 2010. reason.com/archives/2010/03/01/45-swat-raids-per-day

[81] Balko, Radley, *Overkill: The Rise of Paramilitary Police Raids in America* (Washington, DC: Cato Institute, 2006), 1. cato.org/pub_display.php?pub_id=6476

[82] Einstein, Albert, "The World as I See It," *Ideas and Opinions, based on Mein Weltbild*, ed. Carl Seelig, (New York: Bonzana Books, 1954), 8-11.

[83] Miron, Jeffrey A., *The Budgetary Implications of Drug Prohibition* (February 2010), 1. economics.harvard.edu/faculty/miron/files/budgetpercent202010percent20Final.pdf

[84] Wilson, Duff, "U.S. Releases Graphic Images to Deter Smokers," *New York Times,* June 21, 2011. nytimes.com/2011/06/22/health/policy/22smoke.html?_r=1&ref=smokingandtobacco

[85] National Drug Intelligence Center, "Teens and Drugs: Fast Facts, Questions and Answers", NDIC Product No. 2004-L0559-011. justice.gov/ndic/pubs11/12430/index.htm#significant

[86] "Chicago Battles Rise in Teen Murders," *Associated Press,* March 27, 2008.

[87] Degenhardt L, Chiu W-T, Sampson N, Kessler RC, Anthony JC, et al. "Toward a Global View of Alcohol, Tobacco, Cannabis, and Cocaine Use: Findings from the WHO World Mental Health Surveys" *PLoS Medicine* 5(7): July 2008. plosmedicine.org/article/info:doi/10.1371/journal.pmed.0050141#s3

[88] Fox, Maggie, "US Teens Smoke More Marijuana than Tobacco, Says New Survey," *Reuters,* December 14, 2010. csmonitor.com/USA/Latest-News-Wires/2010/1214/US-teens-smoke-more-marijuana-than-tobacco-says-new-survey

[89] Amerigian, Zoë, "Legalizing Marijuana: An Exit Strategy from the War on Drugs," Council on Hemispheric Affairs, April 19, 2011. coha.org/legalizing-pot-an-exit-strategy-from-the-war-on-drugs/

[90] Degenhardt L, Chiu W-T, Sampson N, Kessler RC, Anthony JC, et al. "Toward a Global View of Alcohol, Tobacco, Cannabis, and Cocaine Use: Findings from the WHO World Mental Health Surveys" *PLoS Medicine* 5(7): July 2008. plosmedicine.org/article/info:doi/10.1371/journal.pmed.0050141#s3

[91] Thorton, Mark, "Cato Institute Policy Analysis No. 157: Alcohol Prohibition Was a Failure," Cato Institute, July 17, 1991. scribd.com/fullscreen/31267826

[92] ElSohly MA, Ross SA, Mehmedic Z, Arafat R, Yi B, Banahan BF. "Potency Trends of Δ^9-THC and Other Cannabinoids in Confiscated Marijuana from 1980-1997," *Journal of Forensic Science*

(2000); 45(1):24-30.

[93] Mehmedic, Z., Chandra, S., Slade, D., Denham, H., Foster, S., Patel, A. S., Ross, S. A., Khan, I. A. and ElSohly, M. A., "Potency Trends of Δ⁹-THC and Other Cannabinoids in Confiscated Cannabis Preparations from 1993 to 2008," *Journal of Forensic Sciences*, (2010) 55: 1209–1217.

[94] Schultz, George P. and Paul A. Volcker, "A Real Debate About Drug Policy," *Wall Street Journal*, June 11, 2011.

AFTERWORD

[95] Johnson, Tim, "Mexican Leader Hints Again at U.S. Drug Legalization," *McClatchy Newspapers*, September 20, 2011. mcclatchydc.com/2011/09/20/v-print/124679/mexican-leader-hints-again-at.html